COACHING THE LITTLE LEAGUE®

FIELDER

TEACHING YOUR PLAYERS
to Play Sound, Fundamental Defensive Baseball

MARK GOLA

D1275369

McGraw·Hill

New York   Chicago   San Francisco   Lisbon   London   Madrid   Mexico City
Milan   New Delhi   San Juan   Seoul   Singapore   Sydney   Toronto

Library of Congress Cataloging-in-Publication Data

Gola, Mark.
    Coaching the Little League fielder : teaching your players to play sound,
fundamental defensive baseball / by Mark Gola.— 1st ed.
        p.   cm. — (Little League baseball guide)
    Includes index.
    ISBN 0-07-144302-9
    1. Baseball—Coaching.   2. Little League baseball.   I. Title.   II. Series.

GV875.5.G65   2005
796.357'077—dc22   2004025053

To my parents, Edward F. Gola and Paulette Gola,

the greatest catch a son could ever make

1 2 3 4 5 6 7 8 9 0   DOC/DOC   0 9 8 7 6 5

ISBN 0-07-144302-9

Interior photographs by Michael Plunkett

McGraw-Hill books are available at special quantity discounts to use as premiums and
sales promotions, or for use in corporate training programs. For more information, please
write to the Director of Special Sales, Professional Publishing, McGraw-Hill, Two Penn
Plaza, New York, NY 10121-2298. Or contact your local bookstore.

This book is printed on acid-free paper.

Contents

Acknowledgments   v

Introduction   vii

1   The Defense Never Rests   1

2   Catching and Throwing the Baseball   15

3   Fielding a Ground Ball   29

4   Fielding a Fly Ball   45

5   The Pitcher   57

6   The Catcher   73

7   The First Baseman   91

8   The Third Baseman   105

9   The Second Baseman   121

10   The Shortstop   139

11   The Outfielders   157

12   Team Defense   173

Bibliography   189

Index   191

Acknowledgments

A writer depends on the talents and support of many individuals. To the following, I would like to say thank you:

Mandy Huber, Mark Weinstein, and Heather Taylor of McGraw-Hill, for believing in this concept and for their professional support along the way.

Little League Baseball, for continuing their excellent series of instructional baseball books that help teach the game to coaches and aspiring players.

Thank you to Randy Voorhees for developing the concept for this book and writing the chapter on the pitcher.

Michael Plunkett, photographer, for his excellence behind the camera.

A special thanks to the New Jersey Nitro baseball team from Manalapan, New Jersey, for their participation in the photo shoot. You're an excellent baseball team and a great group of boys: Steven Bacigalupi, Joseph Caputo, Joey Crocco, Alex Decastro, Elliot Drucker, Derek Kawa, Nick Kreiger, Brian Morgan, Timmy Murray, Joseph Ramirez, Richie Ricciardi, and Michael Sette; manager Richard Ricciardi and coaches Steve Kawa, Wayne Kreiger, and Kevin Murray.

Acknowledgments

Stan Davis, my high school baseball coach, for hitting me ground balls in the gym at Toll Gate Elementary School during the winter months.

Sonny Pittaro, my college baseball coach at Rider University, for introducing me to the fact that playing the outfield is not as easy as it looks.

And finally, to several of my friends who help me in a variety of ways: Ed Gola, Randy Voorhees, Dave Gallagher, Norm Coryell, Chad Wallace, and Dave Norris.

Introduction

In the spring of 2004, I was giving a hitting lesson to a young student of the game. His father attended the class, and afterward was venting his frustration about how his Little League baseball team lost a close game to the first-place team in their league. He was particularly bothered because he was convinced that his team had better players and that the top-ranked team, "was nothing special." My first thought was to wonder why this loss still plagued a man of 43 years, but part of my job is to listen, so I did.

"Their hitters weren't that good. We lost the game 4–3, but we should have won 3–2. Two of their runs should never have scored because our right fielder misplayed a ball, and if our catcher doesn't drop a pop-up, we're out of the inning that they scored the game-winning run."

He continued. "They threw two pitchers who didn't throw hard at all and only struck out one batter all game. They might win the regular season, but there is no way they'll win the playoffs."

Two weeks later, I attended a Little League game to watch my friend's son play baseball. They were playing that same first-place team. It was probably the fastest Little League game I'd ever seen, and before you could get up to buy a hot dog, the top team had registered a 3–1 victory.

After the game, I thought about that father's comments, and the word *special*. From an entertainment standpoint, the first-place team wasn't anything special. In fact, you could have described them as downright boring. Their execution was monotonous: ground ball, fielded by the shortstop, one out. Fly ball, right fielder camps under it, two outs. Slow roller, fielded by the third baseman, three outs. There were no titanic blasts off their bats, nor did any pitcher feature a blazing fastball that dominated opposing hitters.

From a baseball standpoint, I thought they were very special. They fielded every routine ground ball, threw the ball accurately, caught fly balls, and backed up bases and teammates. They played terrific defense, and that was precisely why they were a first-place team. Good defense wins baseball games.

Coaching the Little League Fielder is a book dedicated to teaching baseball players how to play good defense. The book covers all aspects of defense, both team and individual, for the youth-level player. *Coaching the Little League Fielder* discusses every conceivable topic under the fielding umbrella: situational positioning, fielding ground balls and fly balls, correct throwing and receiving technique, position-by-position responsibilities, rundowns, and much more.

Playing defense entails more than physical skills. It requires anticipation, quick decisions, aggressiveness, and confidence. These ideals are presented along with teaching proper technique to develop a complete defensive player. A complete player is one who approaches playing defense with mind, body, and glove. Great shortstops, for example, possess certain physical skills, but they also understand where to position themselves, know what they're going to do with the ball before they get it, and, most important, want the ball to be hit to them. Outstanding defensive plays are heavily assisted by the mental preparation that occurs before the pitch is delivered to the plate.

In *Coaching the Little League Fielder*, approximately 125 instructional photographs illustrate the text so that coaches and players have a visual image alongside the explanation of proper technique. Sidebar tips, quotations, and drills also complement the treatment.

Throughout this book, there are many references to players that are written in the form of "he," "his," and "him." This was done only to simplify the presentation of information. Many girls grace Little League baseball diamonds all over the country, and it's my hope that they find this book useful to their development on the field.

The primary objective of a Little League coach is to teach the game of baseball. If each team member develops into a better player than he was at the season's outset, the coaches have done a good job. Wins, regular-season titles, and championships are nice rewards for players, but their improvement is what's most important. Much like adults, children enjoy greater comfort and satisfaction when they see themselves getting better. The rest is just icing on the cake.

And if your team starts playing good defensive baseball as a single unit, perhaps they'll defeat that first-place team 3–2, rather than leaving you scratching your head after a 4–3 defeat.

THE DEFENSE NEVER RESTS

It is often mentioned in baseball circles that good pitching will defeat good hitting. Good defense, however, wins games. Taking away the opposing team's outs stymies their offense and gets your team off the field and into the batter's box. A Little League baseball team is allowed 18 outs per game, and each time an out is recorded, the team bounds one step closer toward securing a victory.

Playing solid defense can help a team in a number of ways. Poor defensive play can hurt a team in an equal number of ways. Positive or negative, the significance of defense to the outcome of ball games is indisputable. In spite of this understanding, defense plays the role of the ugly cousin in the baseball family. Hitting and pitching receive the lion's share of attention and scrutiny. During team workouts, defensive training is often performed during batting practice, as sort of a secondary exercise. Batting averages, pitchers' records, and ERAs (earned run averages) are reviewed and discussed, whereas fielding percentages and team errors committed lack the sensation that would afford them their due. The truth is that a great defense can bail out poor hitting or rescue a pitcher

A baseball team that takes advantage of "out" opportunities will often find itself on the winning end of ball games.

during a shaky outing. Poor defense can waste a productive day at the plate or destroy a masterful pitching performance.

How Good Defense Helps Your Team

Consider this example of a simple play that could happen in any one of the thousands of Little League games played each year. It's the top of the first inning and you're the home team. The pitcher misses the strike zone with the first two pitches and has fallen behind the hitter 2-0. To avoid a 3-0 count, he grooves a fastball down the center of the plate. The hitter (right-handed) rips a foul ball down the left-field line. On the next pitch, the batter puts a perfect swing on the ball and lines a shot toward left center. Your center fielder, surprisingly, is shaded toward the left-center-field gap. He gets a great jump on the ball and makes a running catch for out number one.

First, let's discuss how the center fielder used his head just as much as his legs and glove to make that catch. On the 2-0 count in which the batter pulled the ball foul, the center fielder recognized that the hitter was quick enough to pull the fastball. Instead of standing in the same spot, he put that information to use and adjusted his positioning before the next pitch. Those couple of steps were the difference between a leadoff double and the first out of the inning.

But that catch is so much more than merely being out number one. The pitcher is now facing the second hitter with one out and nobody on base, instead of a runner in scoring position and nobody out. This raises his level of comfort and allows him to focus 100 percent of his efforts on the batter. It also builds his trust in the defense playing behind him, giving him a sense that he needs only to throw strikes and let the batters put the ball in play. The defense will take care of the rest.

Think also of the impact that catch has on the opposing team. It knocks the wind right out of their sails. A sure double to lead off the game that would ignite cheers and excitement suddenly turns into a collective moan followed by the thought, "Uh, oh. I hope it's not going to be one of those days."

The center fielder observed, processed the information, adjusted his positioning, and then applied the fundamentals of catching a fly ball—all simple tasks that were performed within a span of less than 15 seconds. That's playing good defense and that's what it takes to win games. As stated by Hall of Fame shortstop Ozzie Smith, "Good defense means taking momentum away from the team at bat and giving it to your team."

Minimizing the Offense's Chances

During a game, you can expect the opposing team to collect their share of hits and earn a few walks. The good teams, however, minimize the number of chances the offense has to produce runs. When a routine ground ball is hit to an infielder or a fly ball is hit to the outfield, it presents an opportunity for the defense to secure an out. Successful teams capitalize on those opportunities. In doing so, you suffocate the offense until ultimately, their bucket of outs runs empty. They're given only 18 per game. No more and no less.

There are times when you'll read a box score in the newspaper wherein a pitcher throws a complete shutout or gives up just a run, despite giving up seven or eight hits. That is an indication that the defense played an excellent game. On average, the pitcher yielded a hit per inning, but when the defense was given the opportunity to register outs, they did so with consistency. The pitcher gets the "W" by his name, but overall, it's a great defensive effort.

At all levels of baseball, the routine plays in the field are most critical. Spectacular plays are a bonus. You don't expect defensive players to make heart-stopping plays, but they do need to execute the simple putouts. Hall of Fame third baseman Mike Schmidt, who won 10 Gold Gloves for the Philadelphia Phillies, once said, "Show me a great fielder and I'll show you a fielder who makes the routine play."

Big innings occur when the defense gives the offense extra outs—four, five, six in an inning. The base paths become saturated and additional opportunities (at-bats) are presented to the offense. In many ways, baseball is a game of percentages. The more at-bats

To receive credit, the base runner has to touch home plate safely. He can hit, steal, and demonstrate great instinct on the base paths. But a good defense is stingy in allowing opponents to cross home plate.

you give hitters, the more hits they'll accumulate. Take away their outs whenever you can.

An above-average defense also collect outs after the batter has reached base. Keep in mind the base runner has to advance to second base, third base, and then home before a run is tacked onto the scoreboard. This provides more chances for the team in the field to take away outs—and boy, can they make a difference in a game. Outfield assists, force plays, a catcher throwing out a base stealer, and pickoff plays eliminate base runners and detract from that magic number of 18.

Throwing Strikes with Comfort

If you were to ask Little League pitchers to describe their job on the mound, they would probably say that it was "to avoid letting the batter hit the ball." In reality, their approach should be the opposite. It may sound counterintuitive, but pitchers should want hitters to make contact and put the ball into play—because every time the ball leaves the bat, it presents an opportunity for the defense to secure an out.

When pitchers attempt to strike out every hitter, they inevitably throw a lot of pitches. Here are some negative results of pitchers attempting to strike each hitter out:

- The pitcher exits the game earlier than expected. Pitch counts run high and the coach is forced to go to the bullpen. Even if a pitcher were to strike out every hitter, a minimum of three pitches are thrown for each at-bat.
- The pitcher throws a lot of balls out of the strike zone by trying to overthrow or be too precise. Consequently, batters will hit in favorable counts (i.e., 1-0, 2-0, 3-1). Hitting ahead in the count works to the hitter's benefit.

Pitchers are able to focus on throwing strikes when they know they have reliable fielders behind them.

- By running deeper counts, hitters see more pitches. This gives them a big advantage. The more pitches hitters see, the better chance they have of making solid contact.
- Defensive players' concentration weakens as they wait between batted balls. It becomes increasingly difficult to play sharp defense when a lot of time elapses between plays.

Strikeouts are certainly not frowned upon. It is also understood that young players can't be expected to make all the routine plays in the field. As a result, pitchers feel as if they need to personally take care of business to keep the base paths clear. But it's not realistic for pitchers to think they can win a game on their own by striking everyone out. Even Kerry Wood needs the teammates behind him to chalk up victories.

Solid defensive play gives pitchers confidence in their teammates. It allows the pitcher to simply focus on throwing strikes. Again, a ball put into play is an opportunity to record an out. Throwing strikes keeps the game moving, helps the defense stay alert, and minimizes the number of pitches thrown.

Forcing Your Opponent to Adjust

Good defensive teams become a nightmare for opposing hitters. After they have seemingly defeated the pitcher in their one-on-one duel by hitting the ball hard, their personal triumph is short-lived. An infielder or outfielder aptly makes the play and retires the hitter to a seat in the dugout.

When the defense is making plays with regularity throughout a game, hitters begin to think they need to do something more to reach base. This creates tension, which bedevils hitters. They'll overswing and pop pitches up. They'll get overanxious and swing early in the count, relegating themselves to a one- or two-pitch out. They may even attempt to drag bunt, a play that requires perfect execution against a good infield. This sense of urgency to produce hits works heavily in the pitcher's favor. The more hitters try, the more it works against them.

Coaches will also deviate from their customary tendencies when facing a defensive team that shuts down their offense. When a batter reaches base, the coach may quickly call for a steal sign to get that runner in scoring position, fearing another hitter may not reach base for a while. Perhaps that base runner is not the best base stealer, but the coach feels as if the team needs to get something going. As soon as that runner takes off, another opportunity arises for the defense to record an out. Sacrifice bunts, hit-and-run plays, double steals, and suicide squeezes are all signs coaches flash when they are looking to "manufacture" runs. They also provide the defense additional chances to gobble up outs.

Building Pride in Team Play

There is a lot of individualism in baseball. A hitter, for example, stands in the batter's box alone, unable to seek assistance from a team member. When a hitter lines a single to center field, it's his hit and his alone. There are no assists on offense in baseball. There are, however, assists on defense. Good defensive players rely on the reciprocal play of their teammates to record outs. Exceptional defense can develop into a source of team pride.

Playing the field also provides an opportunity for teammates to pick each other up. A shortstop may uncork an errant throw to first but is quickly saved when the first baseman scoops the ball up out of the dirt. A pitcher can throw a high change-up that is clobbered toward the outfield gap, but a right fielder who leaps up and makes an over-the-shoulder catch erases that pitcher's mistake. These are great plays that are not easily accounted for in statistics but are invaluable to a team's success. It's how team chemistry is created.

Good team defense is something players accomplish together.

How Poor Defense Hurts Your Team

Rocky Bridges, a journeyman middle infielder who played in the major leagues from 1951 through 1961, made this statement about the importance of defense: "If you don't catch the ball, you catch the bus." It's a simple, yet profound comment. A team that fails to catch and throw consistently often finds itself on the losing end of ball games.

Extra Outs

Most would agree that the mark of a good hitter is a .300 batting average. A player hitting at a .333 clip is even better than good. Imagine, for a moment, that your team is facing a team whose entire lineup is batting .333. Sounds like your pitching staff is in for a long day, but when you break it down mathematically, it may not appear to be such a daunting task.

A batter hitting .333 gets a hit one out of every three plate appearances. Another way to look at it is that the same batter makes an out two out of every three plate appearances. So if every hitter in the lineup is retired two out of three at-bats, the odds work heavily in the pitcher's (and defensive team's) favor. Out, out, hit. Out, out, hit. Out, out, hit. It's tough to score runs that way.

Obviously, this is not a perfect science. Consecutive hits, extra-base hits, stolen bases, sacrifices, and bases on balls have an impact on how an inning unfolds. But the variable that has a more profound negative impact on run-scoring innings is errors, physical and mental. (Physical errors include bobbling a ground ball, making errant throws, and misjudging fly balls. Mental errors involve failing to cover a base, not backing up a play, throwing to the wrong base, etc.) Granting the offense extra outs crucifies the team in the field. It forces the pitcher to throw more pitches, places more runners on the base paths, and provides the offense with more opportunities to deliver run-producing hits. Keep each inning to three outs and your team will stay in the game.

Stranding the Pitcher

Playing for a team that plays poor defense is a nightmare for a pitcher. Long innings, high pitch counts, and frequent losses are not on any pitcher's wish list. Even worse is that the box score in the newspaper places an "L" next to the pitcher's name in the event of a defeat. Outfielders who miss cutoffs, infielders who drop balls on tag plays, or catchers who allow pass balls never even get a lower case "L" next to their name. The pitcher is credited with the loss and it goes on his personal record.

What is most damaging for young pitchers—even more than receiving a loss—is that they quickly lose faith in their fielders and adopt the belief that they must strike out hitters to get outs. Throwing a well-located pitch that produces a routine ground ball to the shortstop is not good enough, because they don't trust their shortstop will field the ball cleanly and deliver an accurate throw that will be caught by the first baseman. Instead, they have to keep the batter from hitting the ball altogether. To accomplish this, they'll travel one of three paths: (1) They'll try to throw perfect pitches on the outer edges of the strike zone. (2) They'll throw pitches at a higher velocity and blow balls past hitters. (3) They'll fool or deceive hitters with off-speed pitches.

Attempting to be too precise with pitches leads to more pitches thrown out of the strike zone. A greater number of free passes follow along with batters hitting in more favorable counts. Trying to throw harder (overthrowing) diminishes accuracy and accelerates fatigue. Off-speed pitches increase pitch counts because they are much more difficult to throw for strikes. In addition, breaking balls can cause arm soreness or injury if not thrown properly.

11

Pitchers who develop this mentality of trying to strike everyone out suffer long-term as well. They're forced to relearn the correct approach to pitching if they move on to high school or college baseball because they simply won't survive if they don't. Outings will be very short (three or four innings), and their number of walks, hits, and earned runs allowed will skyrocket. Pitchers must learn to trust their defensive teammates and focus on making smart pitches.

When a hitter puts the ball into play, it gives the defense an opportunity to record an out.

Damaging Team Pride

Poor defense can crush team pride and chemistry. What may surface, unfortunately, is finger-pointing and negative banter. Players begin to place blame on other players until it gets to the point where everyone is hoping the ball is not hit to them. When that happens, the team is in deep, deep trouble. Recording an out will seem more complex than nuclear physics.

One of the most important responsibilities of a Little League coach is to prepare the team for competition. To do that, a coach must exercise intelligent judgment when devising practice plans. Kids always want to hit. If it were up to the players, they would hit the entire practice because hitting is fun. And while a coach should always aspire to create an enjoyable playing environment, the right decision is to spend more time at practice on team defense than on anything else. There is no question that hitting is fun, but

It's up to the coaching staff to prepare the team to play defense, so they take the field in a relaxed, confident state of mind.

do you know what is not fun? Trying to withstand an inning where your defense can't get an out. It's tough on the kids going through it, difficult for parents to watch, and heartbreaking for a coach to experience.

Baseball is a sport where the defense must play the game in their minds before it happens. Before each pitch is thrown, every infielder and outfielder must process a litany of "what ifs" to ensure they'll be in the right place or throw the ball to the correct base. "If the ball is hit directly to me I'm throwing it to this base." "If it's hit sharply on the ground to third base I'm going here." "If it's hit to right-center field, if it's a slow tapper to the mound, if the runner steals, if it's a base hit, etc., etc." Once the ball is put into play, the players must now execute the activity they've rehearsed in their mind. To execute efficiently, they must practice it over and over again so they're able to do so without thought. If it's not practiced enough, self-doubt will become a factor and the fielder will buckle under the pressure.

Look out for the well-being of the team and spend the majority of your practice time on defense. The attitude you want to achieve is that every single defensive player wants every ball hit to them because they know they'll make the play. The only way to accomplish this is through countless repetitions during workouts. You may not be the most popular coach during practice, but the smiles on the players' faces will far outnumber the frowns during games.

13

2

CATCHING AND THROWING THE BASEBALL

Catching and throwing the baseball sounds so rudimentary that coaches may elect to skip past these basic skills and focus more on advanced topics. But there are two primary reasons catching and throwing should be taught and practiced regularly. The first is that nothing is more important to a defense than having each member on the field able to throw the ball accurately (with something on it), and catch it consistently. Rundowns, double-play pivots, and pickoffs are examples of plays that are useless to practice if players are unable to catch and throw the ball.

Second, every player on a Little League team, without exception, can stand to improve his throwing and catching technique. Throwing form, in particular, is a skill that most youth players have not mastered. Some throw the ball better than others, but almost none throw it flawlessly. And as for the 1 percent who have perfected throwing, they need to practice it daily to maintain form and continue building arm strength.

As a coach or parent, have you ever a watched a Little League team play catch before a practice or game? It can be a chaotic scene that looks like it came straight out of a Bad News Bears movie.

And this is with stationary targets, positioned a short distance away, with no pressure whatsoever. If players have trouble playing a simple game of catch under these circumstances, what do you think the result will be during game competition? It's essential that they use their time wisely when playing catch. As former Baltimore Orioles shortstop Mark Belanger said, "I never threw a ball without imagining a game situation."

Catching the Ball

The importance of catching throws and batted balls is so obvious that at times it can be overlooked. The pitcher catches the ball thrown back from the catcher and vice versa, the first baseman catches throws from infielders, outfielders catch fly balls off the bat, and infielders catch feeds on force plays. Little League players must

Getting loose before practice or a game is the best time to work on catching and throwing form.

be taught how to properly catch the ball so they're able to do it consistently. They also must be taught to ensure their safety and to catch a ball without fear. Keep in mind that an object (the baseball) is being thrown or hit at them. Human instinct tells them to get out of the way for protection. Young players must overcome that fear first, and then practice perfecting their catching form.

Catching Form

A player should stand in an athletic position, feet slightly farther than shoulder-width apart, knees slightly bent, with the weight on the balls of the feet. The glove is held out in front of the chest, arms nearly at full extension toward the thrower. The throwing hand should rest behind the thumb of the glove. The fingers of the glove are pointed upward and the glove held open as wide as possible to expose the pocket.

When setting up to receive a throw, the player should provide an inviting target by opening his glove and holding it chest-high.

The receiver watches the ball all the way into his glove. This gives the player his best chance of catching the ball clean.

It's very important to teach players to extend the glove out toward the thrower. This allows the player to "see" the ball into the glove, which improves efficiency and also staves off fear. The eyes serve as the protector. If the glove is held in toward the body or off to the side, the eyes lose sight of the ball the last few inches. It's tougher to catch what you can't see, and it becomes a little frightening.

On a perfect throw to the receiver's chest, the player watches the ball all the way into the glove and catches it in the pocket (not the web). Again, the ball is caught out in front of the body. As the ball makes contact with the pocket, the glove hand squeezes and closes the glove. The throwing hand helps close the glove and secures the ball.

On throws that are above the waist and off-center, the glove acts much like a windshield wiper. The palm of the glove remains facing the ball. The arms simply move the glove in a semicircle to the point of the throw. The rest of the body remains stationary. Remind

18

players to keep their head as still as possible so their eyes stay locked on the ball. If there's time (longer or softer throws), they should shift their feet (side to side) to re-center the throw if it's off-target. The more comfortable players become catching the ball, the more they can use their feet to ensure they catch everything in the middle of their body.

Low throws require an adjustment. On balls thrown at or just below the waist, the receiver

To catch a ball thrown to his right, this right-handed player keeps his feet stationary, turns his glove clockwise, and follows the ball into the glove.

should bend at the knees and catch the ball with the glove turned up. When a catch is to be made at the thighs or lower, the player turns the glove over so the fingers point down. The ball should be caught in the pocket or web and the throwing hand clamps down atop the ball to secure it, much like the jaws of an alligator clamp down on its prey.

Low throws often prompt players to quickly turn their glove so that the palm faces up. The first option is to keep the glove pointed up and simply bend at the knees. This position is more efficient, and also brings the eyes closer to the ball.

Catching the ball with two hands is essential for two reasons. It makes the receiver more sure-handed. The ball may jar loose if the glove is not closed in a timely fashion with the second hand acting as a backup. Also, when the ball is caught properly, the throwing hand is in position to remove the ball from the glove for the ensuing throw. The only time a player does not want to catch the ball with two hands is when he has to reach far for a ball very high, very low, or very wide to the right or left. Using two hands in these cases restricts the player's reach and can hinder his ability to catch the ball.

19

Throwing Form

Throwing the ball correctly improves accuracy, maximizes the speed of throws, and diminishes the chance of arm soreness and injury. From a competitive standpoint, throwing the ball efficiently from one teammate to another is a means of recording outs. Outs are what you need to get off the field and into the batter's box to hit.

FEAR FACTOR

Beginner players, whether they're four years of age or eleven years old, are often afraid to catch the ball. As the ball travels on its path, they shift their body away from the ball's path, tuck their head to the side, and hope the ball lands safely in their glove. More often than not, their efforts will be fruitless.

The best way to begin the process of eliminating fear is to practice with a softer ball: an IncrediBall, Hitting Streak ball, tennis ball, or even rolled-up socks. This way, if players make a mistake and are hit with the ball they won't pay the price of a bump or bruise. Also, maintain a close distance (10–20 feet) and toss the ball underhand.

The initial focus must be on keeping the feet planted and the core of the body motionless. This keeps the head still and enables receivers to track the ball with their eyes. Their success rate will immediately improve. Remind the player to extend the glove outward and to "catch" the ball rather than "stab" at it with the glove.

Gradually back up and increase the pace of your underhand tosses. Begin varying the location of the throws center, left, right, higher, lower. When the receiver seems to have improved, move on to light overhand tosses from a short distance. Back up little by little and mark the spot of the longest catch. Utilize this method to turn this drill into a game (i.e., "Today's longest catch was from 34 feet away. Perhaps tomorrow someone will break that mark.") As the players' confidence in their ability rises, their fear will subside. Catching is an acquired skill that takes patience and repetition.

Grip

The correct way to grip the ball is across the seams. Hold the ball so the seams form a reverse "C" (for right-handers). The middle and index finger rest across the top seam so the stitches contact the upper pads of the fingers. The thumb rests against the left side of the ball, and the ring and pinky fingers rest against the right side. The grip should be firm, but not tight. Players should allow some space between the ball and the palm of their hand. The ball should not be jammed into the palm or gripped too tightly as it will diminish velocity and accuracy.

Many Little League players have hands too small to grip the ball with two fingers. If this is the case, they should grip the ball with three fingers (index, middle, and ring fingers). This reduces velocity slightly, but will improve accuracy. The reason for gripping the ball across the seams is that it maximizes the velocity and carry on throws. The objective is to get the ball spinning backward (backspin) as fast as possible, so the seams of the baseball cut through the air to maintain its speed and flight. Gripping the ball with the seams puts the smooth surface of the ball into play, allowing wind resistance to have a greater effect on its flight. A simple example can be demonstrated with pitching. A four-seam fastball (gripping the ball across the seams) generates the most velocity. A two-seam fastball (gripping the ball with the seams) manufactures the most movement. Infielders and outfielders want to throw four-seam fastballs from their positions, not two-seamers.

21

Separation/Power Position

To initiate the throw, the non-throwing-side foot takes a small step directly toward the target. The body turns to align itself with the target. The shoulders should be in a direct line with the teammate receiving the throw. As the step is taken, the ball is taken out of the glove and the arm

The four-seam grip is the preferred grip when throwing the ball from the infield or outfield. It produces the straightest, fastest throw.

swings down, reaches back, and reaches up in a fluid motion. When the ball is raised upward, it should face away from the target. (Example: If you were standing on the pitcher's mound facing the batter's box, the ball would face center field.) Cupping the ball so it faces the target is a common mistake. The step and backswing occur simultaneously, and this is often referred to as "separation." The stride goes in one direction and the ball (or armswing) moves in the opposite direction.

The glove arm extends out and points at the target. The throwing arm continues to move upward until the elbow rises above the shoulder. Having the glove arm extended out at shoulder-height and the throwing-arm elbow held above the shoulder with the ball

This player poses in the power position. The ball is faced away from the target, and the elbow is raised above the shoulder. The glove extends out and shoulders are aligned to the receiver.

faced away is called the "power position." From this position, the player is primed to accelerate his arm forward and fire a throw.

The Throw

The first movement is not with the throwing arm, but rather the glove arm. It begins to pull in toward the body as the throwing-arm shoulder begins to externally rotate. An image to give players that emphasizes the glove-arm action is to have them imagine they're elbowing someone behind them. The throwing arm then accelerates forward, keeping the elbow elevated higher than the shoulder. The ball is released at the one o'clock or two o'clock position. (A twelve o'clock release point would be straight over the head, and a three o'clock release point would be sidearm.) The arm continues forward, then down and across the body and finishes across the opposite-side leg. The momentum of the throwing arm carries the throwing-side leg forward.

A common mistake youth players make is that they drop their elbow below their shoulder and throw sidearm. This diminishes velocity and accuracy. They may get away with throwing sidearm on short throws, but they'll suffer on longer throws.

When players attempt to throw the ball harder, they often vary the movements preceding the throw. For example, they will take a longer stride, tilt back and lower their rear shoulder, or grip the ball tighter. All of these types of movements diminish speed and accuracy. The mechanics of the throw always remain the same. To throw the ball harder, players simply increases their arm speed (forward) after they have reached the power position. Arm speed is what makes the ball travel fast. There may be flaws in the preceding mechanics that hinder arm speed, such as blocking off the hips by striding too far closed, but from the proper position arm acceleration is what generates velocity.

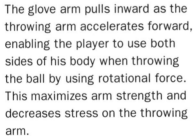

The glove arm pulls inward as the throwing arm accelerates forward, enabling the player to use both sides of his body when throwing the ball by using rotational force. This maximizes arm strength and decreases stress on the throwing arm.

The throwing arm finishes across the body.

The distance of the throw dictates the length of the backswing. Outfielders employ a longer backswing because their throws generally have to travel a greater distance. Infielders have shorter throws and also have less time to release the ball, so a shorter backswing is required.

Throwing Accurately

Much like consistent hitting, accurate throwing is relative to the degree of a player's hand-to-eye coordination. Many players throw with incorrect form, off-balance, or on the run, and somehow manage to hit their target. Not all is lost when perfect form is not exercised. Fielders can still make an accurate throw if they focus on their target and execute with confidence.

Shrinking the Target

A mistake many players make is that they're very liberal in setting their sights on a target. A shortstop may field a ground ball and attempt to throw the ball to the first baseman. That may sound logical, but the target needs to be more specific. If you set out to throw the ball to a general area, that is exactly what you'll do—throw the ball to a general area.

The target needs to be more detailed. Perhaps the shortstop could instead seek to throw the ball to the first baseman's upper body, or directly at the first baseman's glove. Many accurate infielders will be so specific that they'll select a letter on the front of their first baseman's jersey and try to hit that with their throw. Training oneself to be precise with throws can greatly improve accuracy. If the shortstop misses the "J" on the jersey, perhaps he'll hit the "R." When throwing to a general area, if he misses the first baseman, he'll earn himself an "E."

Throw It, Don't Aim It

A player's accuracy is at its best when the ball is thrown with confidence and authority. Accuracy (and velocity) suffers if a fielder attempts to guide a ball to the target. When a player fires a throw, the body stays loose and the actions remain athletic. If a throw is aimed, the body tenses up and the muscles contract. This reduces arm speed, adversely affecting the pace and consistency of the throw.

Erratic throws will happen during a baseball season, as will faulty swings and wild pitches. Defensive players must understand that it's okay to make mistakes in the field, as long as they are aggressive mistakes. A good coach should never be upset or disappointed with an aggressive mistake. It's apprehension or timid play in the field that must be addressed as an issue of concern. Play defense to make plays, not to avoid mistakes.

Drills

One-Knee Drill

This is an excellent exercise for developing proper throwing technique. Place the knee of your post leg (right knee for a right-handed player) on the ground with your stride foot flat on the ground for balance. Hold your glove directly in front of your chest with your hand holding the ball in your glove. Rotate your shoulders and separate into the power position. Now deliver the throw, making sure to extend your throwing arm down and across your stride leg and to pull your glove arm down and into your side. From a distance of approximately 20 feet, the player should throw 15–20 balls during this drill.

Game of 21

Playing catch allows players to get loose and build arm strength. Accuracy, however, is often the forgotten element of focus. The game of 21 increases a player's concentration on throwing accurately.

Pair two players and place them 30 to 40 feet apart. The targets are an imaginary rectangle formed at the top and bottom of the partner's shoulders and waist, and an imaginary rectangle around the partner's head. If a throw arrives within the chest rectangle, score a point. If it comes within the head boundaries, score two points. The first player to get to 21 points wins the game.

Long Toss

Long toss is a drill used for building arm strength. Begin playing catch from approximately 40 feet, and back up five feet every five throws. Continue moving back until you reach 70 feet. (Players with stronger arms may even be able to move back to 90 feet.) During the latter stages of this drill, do not unleash high, arcing throws. Keep the ball on a straight line. If you can no longer reach your partner in the air, do so on one bounce.

3

FIELDING A GROUND BALL

Coaches train pitchers to throw the ball down in the strike zone. The lower they locate their pitches, the better chance the hitter will produce a ground ball. And ground balls lead to outs.

When a ball is hit on the ground, friction reduces its pace. The grass or dirt slows the ball, giving fielders more time to get into a position to intercept it, glove it, and throw it to a teammate for an out. A ball hit above the ground (line drives and fly balls) encounters only the air, allowing the baseball to run its course with minimal interruption. These hits have a greater chance of finding real estate safely, sometimes for extra-base hits. Ground balls generally result in outs or, at worst, base hits.

So if the pitcher does his job of keeping the ball down and getting batters to hit the ball on the ground, it's essential that his defense is able to field ground balls. And not just a select few

The majority of batted balls in Little League are hit on the ground. Good defensive teams are proficient at gloving balls off the ground.

infielders, but every player. It's just as important that the right fielder be efficient at fielding grounders as it is the shortstop. Ground balls lead to outs, and the defense must be poised and prepared to take advantage.

Positioning

Coaches expend most of their energy teaching the proper technique for fielding a ground ball, and rightfully so. But positioning is also a subject that must be addressed. After all, a fielder has to be able to get to a ground ball in order to apply proper technique. If not, execution of the fundamentals will never even come into play.

The art of fielding a ground ball begins before the pitcher even initiates his windup. First, the fielder must assume the ball will be hit to him. Every defensive player, including the pitcher and catcher, should anticipate having the ball hit to them and understand where that play is to be made.

Exactly where each player should stand at position is not random. Several factors must be taken into consideration when making an educated guess as to where to shade: to the left, right, deep, or shallow. Is the hitter likely to pull the ball or hit it to the opposite field? Where is the catcher setting up for the pitch (location)? Does the pitcher have his good fastball? Is the catcher calling for an off-speed pitch? What is the score? What inning is it? How many outs are there?

It sounds like a lot, but all of these variables must be considered. Many successful infielders and outfielders increase their range with knowledge. Quickness and speed are God-given assets, but calculated anticipation is an intangible that can be acquired through observation and attentiveness.

Indicators that a hitter is more likely to pull the ball:

- Hits in the middle of the lineup: 3, 4, or 5
- Excellent bat speed
- Top hand heavy with his swing (rolls his top hand early)
- Early or ahead in the count
- Timing is early (out in front of pitches)
- Stride foot steps open (away from home plate)
- Pitcher throws a fastball at an average to below-average velocity
- Pitcher is throwing an off-speed pitch
- Catcher is set up over the middle to inside part of the plate

Indicators that a hitter is more likely to hit the ball to the opposite field:

- Hits late in the lineup: 7, 8, or 9
- Slow bat or long swing
- Inside-out swing (lead arm dominates his swing)
- Two strikes in the count
- Stride foot steps closed (toward home plate)
- Pitcher throws an above-average fastball
- Catcher is set up over the outside part of the plate

Teach fielders to check or adjust their positioning on each pitch, not just batter to batter. Stress the importance of extracting information during a hitter's at-bat. Has the hitter pulled a fastball foul? The defense should take a step or two to the pull side of the field. Is the batter taking defensive swings? The defense should shift to the opposite-field side and the outfield may want to take a few steps in.

Explain these factors to your defense and train them to adjust their positioning on their own. If the coaching staff is constantly moving them without explanation, the players will never learn and will simply rely on adults to do the thinking for them. If they learn to do it, coaches won't have to constantly shout a command, which enables them to focus on other aspects of the game.

Preparation

It's not enough to be standing in the right spot. The fielders must prepare themselves on each pitch. Getting into the "ready position" enables players to react quickly and athletically.

The ready position is similar to that of a basketball player playing defense or of a tennis player awaiting a serve. The feet are positioned slightly farther than shoulder-width apart. Knees are bent and the rear end is down a bit. The player is balanced on the balls of the feet with a slight forward lean. The glove is held out approximately waist-high, spread open with the palm facing upward. Do not allow the players to place their glove and hand on their knees. The first thing they'll need to do when the ball is hit is pull the glove off their knee and move it out in front of them. This takes time.

As the pitcher is about to release the ball, the player should take a "creeper step" toward home plate. The step can be taken with the left or right foot, depending on the player's comfort. Regardless of which foot is used, a creeper step is important because it keeps the weight on the balls of the feet and the player's momentum moving forward. If players stand flat-footed, the tendency is for them to fall back on their heels when fielding the ball. Many individuals have heard the expression, "Don't let the ball play you." This is precisely what happens when a fielder's weight falls back on his heels. A creeper step helps stave off this common field-ing mistake.

Fundamentals of Fielding a Ground Ball

There are four simple steps to fielding a routine ground ball. Play-ers who practice these steps will experience consistent success field-ing ground balls cleanly. Listed here are the four steps, followed by a brief description of each.

1. Gain ground and center the ball.
2. Reach for the ball in the fielder's position.
3. Relax the hands and absorb the ball with "touch."
4. Look the ball all the way into the glove.

Gain Ground and Center the Ball

Gaining ground simply means to move forward to the ball after it is hit. Rather than sit back and wait for the ball, the fielder takes steps in. This accomplishes two things: First, the fielder will get to the ball quicker and shorten the distance of the throw. This gives the player more time to set his feet and increases the chances of an accurate throw. Second, it reduces the risk of falling back on the heels when fielding the ball. Moving forward keeps the weight on the balls of the feet, allowing for a slightly forward lean when preparing the glove.

Not every ball is hit directly at the fielder, so fielders must first center the ball in order to field the ball in the middle of their body. Fielding the ball in the middle of the body maximizes the distance a fielder can reach for the ball, and it provides a backstop should the ball take a bad hop. In addition, it's easier to see the ball into the glove when it's directly in front of the eyes. If it's off to the side, the eyes may lose sight of the ball prematurely.

The best infielders attack ground balls. This player charges forward first and then sets up to field the ball.

This enables the infielder to field the ball sooner and shortens his throw to first base.

Reach for the Ball in the Fielder's Position

A player in the basic fielder's position should use a wide base such that the knees are set just outside shoulder-width. The feet are set square or the glove-side foot is positioned slightly ahead of the throwing-side foot.

When setting up to field a ground ball, players bend at the knees and lower their rear end. This is extremely important. It allows the fielder to remain in an agile position and to reach out for the ball. Commonly, young players incorrectly bend at the waist, making them flat-footed and unable to extend the glove out front.

The glove extends out, hand and wrist relaxed. The fingertips of the glove touch the ground, but the rest of the glove hovers above

This player is set up in the basic fielder's position. His knees are bent and rear end lowered to the ground. He has centered the ball and reaches out with his glove to receive the ball with two hands.

ground (like a shovel). Make sure the glove is held wide open. The throwing hand is held just to the side of the glove, allowing the ball to enter the pocket.

Relax the Hands and Absorb the Ball

As the ball enters the glove, the hands and arms lightly retract in toward the body to "give" with the ball. If the hands and arms are too stiff, the ball may jar and escape the glove. The ball should be absorbed into the glove. Fielders can imagine they're catching an egg and trying to avoid breaking it. The throwing hand then covers the ball to secure and quickly grip it.

Look the Ball All the Way In

Fielders often get into perfect position and at the last moment pull their head up out of nervousness. People instinctually get their head out of harm's way, so fielders must be trained to keep their head (and eyes) down when gloving a ground ball. One method of teaching players to keep their head down is to ask that they count the number of bounces the ball takes on its path to the glove. In order to count every bounce, they must watch it all the way into the glove.

Another reason players pick their head up prematurely is that they want to see how far the runner is from the base. Stress the point that making a play on a ground ball has two steps: (1) field-

When a ground ball is far to the player's glove-side, he should make an athletic play. He fields the ball outside of his glove-side foot.

ing the ball; (2) throwing the ball. You can't accomplish step two unless you successfully execute step one. Field it first, and then get yourself into position to make an accurate throw.

Backhand Plays

The backhand is used when fielders do not have time to get their body in front of the ball. Hard-hit balls just to the player's non-glove side or slower hit balls several steps in that direction call for the backhand play.

We'll assume the fielder is right-handed when explaining backhand techniques. The backhand play can be fielded off (just outside of) the left foot or just inside of the right foot. The pace and distance to the right of the hit often dictates which foot the ball is fielded to. Most players have a preference (right foot or left foot), but there will be situations when the play happens so fast there isn't time to set up to the preferred foot. Infielders should practice fielding backhands off both the right and left foot.

Outside the Left Foot

This technique is more frequently used for deep backhand plays that require longer throws. When fielding off the left foot, the final step is a crossover step, left over right. The fielder bends deep at the knees to lower his body to the ball. He then turns his glove over and reaches across his body. The glove, open as wide as possible, is held just in front of the left foot. The fingers point down and graze the dirt, palm facing the ball. The infielder keeps his nose behind the glove and attempts to catch the ball in the webbing, rather than the palm. Once in position, he watches the ball into the glove and squeezes it shut as the ball enters.

After the ball is received, fielders have two options for how to make the throw with regard to their footwork. If it's a play where

The shortstop makes a backhand play outside his left foot. Notice he bends deep at the knees as he receives the ball.

38

they've stopped their momentum right before fielding the ball, they can rise up, turn their body toward the target, step with the left foot to the base they're throwing, and fire. If their momentum is still moving right, they should take an extra step and plant their right foot, turn to the target, step with the left foot, and throw. Planting with the right foot provides a strong base to gather balance before unleashing a long throw.

Inside the Right Foot

This technique is more frequently used for backhand plays that require shorter throws. To execute the backhand play inside the right foot, the final step is a jab step with the right foot. Bend deep at the knees and reach to field the ball just inside the right foot. After the ball is fielded, push up off the right foot to gather bal-

On balls hit deep to the backhand side, the infielder needs to think less about footwork and more about getting to the ball.

ance. Transfer the ball from glove to hand, step toward the target, and throw. This method is also preferable in double-play situations on a ball hit to the third baseman or shortstop. It takes less time and is conducive to shorter throws.

Bending deep at the knees is critical whether the player is fielding outside the left foot or inside the right. Players commonly bend at the waist, which makes this play much more difficult. For starters, it's not an athletic position from which to make a tough play. Furthermore, the eyes are farther from the ball and the glove often doesn't quite reach the ground, allowing the ball to slip underneath or bounce off the glove's fingertips. Players should be reminded to bend deep at the knees as they reach for the ball.

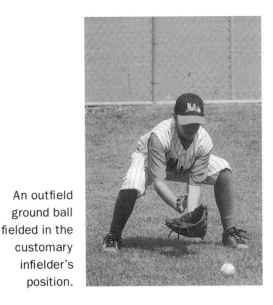

An outfield ground ball fielded in the customary infielder's position.

Outfield Ground Balls

Outfielders are usually associated with fly balls, but when a ball is driven through the infield, it's the outfielder who must field the ball off the ground. There are three methods of fielding a ground ball in the outfield. The game situation dictates what type is used.

Infielder's Position

With runners on base or a fast runner at the plate, an outfielder should charge the ball and field it like an infielder. Run quickly at the ball to eat up ground, break down to set up like an infielder as the ball nears, field it, and fire the ball to the cutoff man or base. Additionally, the ball must be retrieved and returned to the infield quickly to keep runners from taking an extra base.

An outfield ground ball fielded in the one-knee position.

One-Knee Position

With nobody on base, or if the ball is hit extremely hard, the outfielder should go down to one knee to field the ball. A right-handed outfielder puts his right knee on the ground. His left foot is flat on the ground, and his glove is held in the middle of the body. The fielder should lean slightly forward and glove the ball with two hands. This is the safest way to ensure the ball does not get past the outfielder and roll to the fence.

This method is also suggested in late innings when you want to keep the batter off of second base. A base hit that is bobbled or kicked by the outfielder presents an opportunity for the hitter to advance to second base.

Do or Die

This method of fielding a ground ball is used by outfielders who are trying to keep a runner from advancing or, more likely, scoring a run. For example, with the game tied and a runner on second base, the outfielder must charge a base hit as quickly as possible to attempt to hold or throw out the runner. The do-or-die method is used in these situations.

An outfield ground ball fielded in the do-or-die position.

Upon the ball being hit, the outfielder should immediately align himself so he's charging the ball on a direct line toward the base he's throwing. If he's throwing home and the ball is hit to his left, he must run laterally to the left first, before charging forward. The player should run full speed at the ball. As the ball nears, the outfielder reaches down with his glove and fields the ball just in front and to the side of his glove-side foot. The ball is fielded with glove only, not two hands. Once the ball is in the glove, the outfielder quickly changes the ball to his throwing hand, taking the fewest number of steps possible before releasing the throw. Remember, for every step an outfielder takes, the base runner is taking two.

Drills

Ground Balls Off the Wall

The only things necessary for this drill are a ball, glove, wall, and the desire to improve. Throw the ball against the wall, shuffle your feet to get in front of it, and field the ground ball with an emphasis on proper technique. As the ball is fielded, quickly shift your feet and align yourself for the next throw. Vary the height of your throws to create different types of ground balls.

ADVANCED METHOD: FIELDING THROUGH THE BALL

An advanced method of fielding ground balls and throwing to first base is to keep the feet moving and field through the ball. This is a technique commonly practiced by shortstops.

Instead of charging the ball and breaking down into the fielder's position, the player takes an angle around the ball that has him fielding the ball with momentum toward first base. He slows down on his approach but his feet keep moving as the ball is gloved. The glove-side foot is slightly forward, and the ball is fielded just off-center toward his right foot (for right-handers).

Derek Jeter is the perfect example of a shortstop who frequently uses this fielding technique. The fielder gets to the ball quicker, reduces the distance of the throw, and has momentum going toward first base on the throw. Jeter rarely has to show off his strong arm, because he eats up so much ground and has momentum going toward first base.

Field 25 ground balls per session. Soft hands and quick feet are marks of a good fielder. The better you get, the more you should challenge yourself to increase range. A variation of this drill is to throw balls to the right and left and work on backhand plays and fielding the ball off your glove-side foot.

Pickups

A coach, parent, or player stands approximately 10 feet away with a baseball. The player is set in the fielder's position. The feeder rolls the ball a few feet to the player's right. The player shuffles his feet to the right, fields the ball, and tosses it underhand back to the feeder. The feeder then rolls the ball a few feet to the player's left. The player shuffles his feet, fields the ball, and tosses it underhand back to the feeder. This continues back and forth until the player has fielded 25 pickups.

Count the Bounces

Little League players often pull their head up prematurely when fielding a ground ball. To try to fix this problem, request that players count the number of bounces the ball takes before reaching their glove. The players set up for the ground ball, count the bounces while the ball is on its path, field the ball, and call out the number as they throw the ball back.

To add aggressiveness to this drill, challenge players to field each ball before a certain number of bounces occur. You might say, for example, "The ball has to be fielded before it takes four bounces." This forces them to charge the ball.

4

FIELDING A FLY BALL

In theory, fly balls offer the simplest chance of recording an out. One of the nine players in the field must catch the ball before it hits the ground. That's it. By contrast, a strikeout requires three strikes within an at-bat. And when a ground ball is hit, a fielder must glove the ball cleanly and throw it accurately to a teammate before the runner gets to the base; then the teammate must catch the throw while holding the base, or quickly apply a tag to the incoming runner for an out. But when a ball is hit in the air, a player only has to catch the ball out of the air. Accomplishing this simple task tacks an out on the scoreboard instantaneously.

In reality, Little League coaches and parents know that catching fly balls can be an adventure. They also realize that when a ball leaves the bat airborne, it has the ingredients of an extra-base hit, warranted or unwarranted. Why do youth players have so much difficulty catching fly balls? Is the technique that complex? No it isn't. In fact, it's very simple. However, there are two factors that play a much greater role than technique: fear and judgment.

Eliminating Fear

When something falls out of the sky, people are taught to run for cover. In baseball, kids are asked to position themselves so that they

Catching fly balls is integral to playing good team defense.

stand directly under the falling object. To eliminate that instinctual fear, players must be eased into the behavior through repetition. Toss balls underhand from short distances and gradually increase the height. Once a degree of comfort has been reached, begin to throw overhand pop-ups before eventually hitting balls off the bat.

Should players still exhibit fear, use IncrediBalls, tennis balls, or even rolled-up socks. They simply may be afraid of being hit by a hardball. Take that factor out of the equation and practice technique with a softer ball. The better they become, the more comfortable and confident they will be. Slowly mix in hardballs as they progress.

The other type of fear that infiltrates the minds of young players is a fear of failure. They realize that if they do not catch a fly ball, it will result in something greater than a "one-base error." This causes players to approach fly balls tentatively. They "hope" to catch the ball, rather than aggressively pursuing a chance for an out. The number-one remedy for this fear of failure is taking fly ball after fly ball. Repetition achieves improvement, comfort, and confidence.

Developing Judgment

Good judgment of fly balls allows players to quickly run to and arrive at the point of the ball's descent. Do I run to the right or left, and even more difficult, do I run in or back? If an outfielder is unable to get to the spot where the ball falls, all the superior technique in the world is not going to matter. Developing judgment is critical to becoming a proficient outfielder.

The best way to improve judgment is to field countless fly balls on a daily (or at least semidaily) basis. This is true for both Little League players and major-league players. Hitting fly balls to infielders and outfielders is something coaches often forget to incorporate into their practice schedule. Players must see balls in the air to get better at judging and catching them.

The optimum time for infielders and outfielders to work on fly balls is during batting practice. A ball hit by a batter facing live pitching accurately simulates what the defense will encounter during a game. Players commonly goof around or engage in conversation during batting practice. Emphasize the importance of treating it like an actual ball game and their judgment and execution will improve.

Catching a Fly Ball

The proper technique for catching a fly ball is simple. The fingers of the glove point toward the sky. The glove is held to the right or left of the outfielder's head, depending on comfort and on what side the ball is hit. Make sure players do not block their eyes with their glove. The eyes are their protector and mustn't be obstructed. The eyes follow the ball all the way down and into the glove's pocket. Fly balls are always caught with two hands, unless the player is making a running catch and reaches for the ball.

48

At an early age, players should be trained to catch the ball over their throwing shoulder (whenever possible). This places them in position to catch, reach into their glove for the ball, and

A great catch in the outfield can change the momentum of a game.

QUICK TIPS FOR OUTFIELDERS

- Check the wind each inning. Wind influences the flight of the ball.
- Pay attention to who is at the plate (i.e., strong hitter, weak hitter, pull hitter, slap hitter).
- Know how many steps you are from the outfield fence.
- If a ball slices or hooks, it will always hit with a curve toward the foul line.
- Know what you're going to do with the ball before it is hit.

quickly throw it back to the infield. This is an advanced skill for Little League players, but if they get into the habit early, it's one less thing they'll have to learn as they progress.

On balls that players must run in (forward) to catch, they should turn their glove over (fingers pointed down) only if they have to catch the ball below their waist. In all other cases, keep the fingers pointed up or slightly to the side. On balls above the shoulders, the glove acts like a windshield wiper, arcing back and forth depending on the ball's location.

Going Back on Fly Balls

Anyone who has been to a Little League game has witnessed this

On routine fly balls, an outfielder catches the ball with two hands over his throwing shoulder. Using two hands secures the ball and also simplifies transferring the ball from glove to hand.

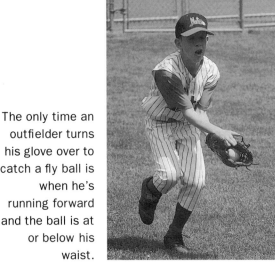

The only time an outfielder turns his glove over to catch a fly ball is when he's running forward and the ball is at or below his waist.

occurrence. A ball is hit in the air. The outfielder first freezes and then begins to backpedal. With his glove raised as high in the air as possible, he continues to backpedal only to have the ball land safely over his head for an extra-base hit. Make no mistake, going back on fly balls is not easy, but it's certainly not impossible. The first step to making this play is literally the first step. Players must learn to employ a drop step.

Drop Steps

A drop step is the first step taken on a deep fly ball. Say, for example, the ball is hit over the fielder's right shoulder. The initial step is a drop step with the right foot. The outfielder lifts the right foot off the ground, swings back, and "points the toe to where he wants to go." This opens the hips and enables the outfielder to run on a direct path to the ball.

On a ball hit over the outfielder's left shoulder, he takes a drop step with the left foot. He runs a direct path to the ball and tries to beat the ball to the spot. It's much easier for a player to catch a fly ball when he's camped under it rather than when he's still on the run. Teach your outfielders to beat the ball to the spot instead of coasting for it.

Outfielders must learn to turn their back on fly balls when chasing them down. They'll cover more ground when turning their back and running to a spot as opposed to coasting sideways and following the ball with their eyes the entire way. Turning their back on the ball takes time for players to learn and perform because inexperienced outfielders will be afraid to take their eyes off the ball. However, it increases range dramatically when they learn to trust their judgment and run to the spot. On deep fly balls, outfielders should turn their back, run, and occasionally glance back to make sure their path to the ball is on target.

Last, teach outfielders to run on their toes when chasing fly balls to their right and left. This keeps the head and eyes still, making it easier to track the ball. Some outfielders mistakenly land on their heels as they run, which causes their head to bounce. The ball bounces in their sight, making the play more difficult.

The Outfield Fence

Everyone fears running into a fence, especially a child 12 years of age or younger. To minimize that fear, there are steps that can be taken by the outfielder and his teammates. Work with players going back on balls near the fence in terms of safety measures as well as execution.

While going back on balls, the outfielder correctly turns his back to the ball. This enables him to see how far he has to go before reaching the fence. However, the outfielder continuously glances back to make sure he's on path to catch the ball. As he prepares to make the catch, the eyes remain on the ball even though he still may be moving back. This is the part that can be scary for outfielders and even dangerous.

On this play the outfielder extends his throwing arm to feel for the fence and protect himself from crashing into it. Once his hand touches the fence, he knows he's out of room. If he's chasing a ball that is to his glove side, he has to do his best to quickly glance or use his glove arm to determine how much room he has left before reaching the fence.

From the set position, the outfielder drops back to open his hips.

He then runs back to the point of the ball's descent and reaches up to make a running catch.

The best protection is another pair of eyes. Fellow outfielders must be vocal and communicate what they see. When the outfielder has room going back, his teammates should yell, "You've got room! You've got room!" to calm his nerves. If he's coming close, they should also let him know by calling, "Fence! Fence!" Once he hears that, he stops his pursuit and plays the ball off the fence.

He runs a step or two past the point of descent, turns to face the ball, and makes a catch with two hands over his throwing shoulder.

On deep fly balls, the outfielder extends his throwing arm to "feel" for the fence. He should also listen for calls from his fellow outfielders that let him know if he has room or not.

Drills

Underhand/Overhand Fly Balls

This drill is used to teach proper technique and eliminate the element of fear. Standing 30 feet away, toss balls underhand approximately 15 to 20 feet in the air. The player should focus on moving to the point of the ball's descent, getting into proper position, and catching the ball with two hands. The player's head (and eyes) remain still, locked on the ball. Gradually move back and toss balls overhand. Increase the height of the throws as the player's comfort and confidence build.

Quarterback/Wide Receiver

The coach or parent plays quarterback and the outfielder plays wide receiver. On the call of "Hike!" the player sprints out a des-

The wide-receiver drill. The coach gives the player a pattern to run and hits him with a pass.

ignated pattern. The tosser lofts the ball in the air so the outfielder catches the ball on the run. Vary the pass patterns, running straight back, diagonal, lateral cuts, and so on. Remind outfielders to run on their toes, not their heels.

Fly Balls Coming In

Stand approximately 60 to 80 feet from the outfielder. Call out, "Break!" and the player sprints toward you at full speed. Toss the ball (at varying heights) so the player must catch the ball below the waist. The outfielder's glove should be pointed down so the fingers point to the ground. This is a tough play for the outfielder to make but a drill that players enjoy.

5

THE PITCHER

The primary responsibility of a pitcher is to throw the ball over the plate. Once the ball is released, the pitcher becomes a fielder. A pitcher should understand that being good in the field will produce more outs and more wins. That is all the incentive he'll need to become a good "glove man" on the mound.

Anticipation, Observation, and Communication

The first key to being a good defensive pitcher is to anticipate what's going to happen before it does. A pitcher should always anticipate that the ball is going to be hit to him. The second thing he should do is anticipate what to do with the ball once it's caught. By predetermining future actions, a pitcher will be able to act swiftly and decisively once the ball is fielded. If the pitcher is not directly involved in a play he should observe the runners and make a decision about who should field the ball, where it should be thrown, and where fielders should position themselves.

Communication is another key element in good fielding. Communication takes place before and during the play. For example, with a runner on first and less than two outs, a pitcher must communicate before the pitch with his middle infielders regarding who

Anytime there is a potential force play at second base, the pitcher must communicate with the middle infielders to determine who is covering second base. A simple, "Me and you," between the pitcher and middle infielder (before the pitch) can eliminate any confusion.

will be covering second base if a ground ball is hit back to the mound. An example of communication during the play is when the catcher is fielding a bunt. Because the catcher's head is down to field the ball, the pitcher must become the "eyes" of the play. The pitcher yells in a loud, clear voice telling the catcher which base to throw the ball to or, in some cases, to not throw the ball at all.

58

The pitcher is the centerpiece of the defense. Consider these facts:

- The pitcher plugs the biggest hole in the infield.
- A good fielding pitcher takes away the bunt from the opposition's offensive game plan.
- The pitcher initiates many double plays.
- The pitcher becomes the first baseman on certain ground balls to the right side of the field.
- The pitcher fields some infield pop-ups and directs traffic on others.
- The pitcher backs up bases on throws from the outfield (he is the last line of defense).
- The pitcher covers home on passed balls and wild pitches with a runner on third.
- The pitcher participates in rundown plays.

The bottom line is that the pitcher must be a leader on defense, both before and after the ball is thrown. Every opportunity to secure an out is important, so the pitcher must be an active participant who uses his brain, his eyes, his mouth, and his glove just as much as his arm.

Fielding Ground Balls and Line Drives

As the fielder (in fair territory) closest to the batter, the pitcher has the least amount of time available to react to a ball hit at him. The pitcher must finish in a position that allows him to defend himself and his position or plenty of unnecessary hits will be surrendered, and a few bruises will be sustained along the way as well. The pitcher must be in position to field the ball as his back leg hits the ground.

Here are a few checkpoints. Pitchers should have their

- Weight on the balls of their feet
- Weight evenly balanced
- Glove held up (fingers to the sky) and open
- Eyes up and directed toward the hitting zone

The good news about being the fielder closest to the batter is that when the pitcher fields the ball there is plenty of time to throw the batter or runner out.

Ground Ball with the Bases Empty

The "comebacker" is the ball hit right back to the pitcher. If the ball can be caught cleanly, the pitcher should do so. If not, the pitcher should knock it down with the glove or body. Remember, there is plenty of time to throw the runner out, because the hitter has barely left the batter's box by the time the ball reaches the mound. And there isn't any runner, no matter how fast, who can outrun the ball. One caveat: pitchers should never try to knock the ball down with their bare hand. One out isn't worth risking serious injury. Use the glove or body to knock the ball to the ground.

Ground Ball with Runners on Base

When there are runners on base, the pitcher must know which base to throw to when fielding a ground ball. This is especially important when the double play is in order. First, there must be communication with the fielders. The pitcher should tell them exactly what he plans to do when the ball is fielded. Where the ball is thrown depends upon the situation. In all the following situations, assume that there are less than two outs and you're playing the pitcher's position.

Runner on First

Ideally you want to throw the ball to second base to get the lead runner, the beginning of a double play. The majority of the time, the shortstop will be covering second base. As the pitcher, square your shoulders, step to the target, and throw the ball chest-high and over the base. Do not attempt to lead the fielder to the base! Trust that he'll do his job and get to the base. The only time you should throw to first base in this situation is if the ball is slowly hit to your left or right, or if you bobble the ball, or if you're protecting a big lead and want to make sure of an easy out.

After the pitch is delivered to home plate, the pitcher becomes an additional defender. A good fielding pitcher can help himself out of a jam.

On a force play to second base, the pitcher must take the time to square his feet and gain balance. Errant throws on this play are often caused by failing to set the feet and rushing the throw.

DON'T BE A HERO

If your pitcher happens to be struck by a line drive or hard ground ball, be realistic about whether or not he should continue pitching in that game. Any injury that causes the pitcher to change the mechanics of his delivery is serious enough that he should be removed from the game. Altering pitching mechanics could cause further injury to the pitching arm. Also, a change in the mechanics could become a hard habit to break. Remove the pitcher from the game to get the injury treated, and don't attempt to pitch him until his body allows him to use the good mechanics that made him an effective pitcher in the first place. All coaches love tough pitchers, those who want to stay in the game, no matter what. But when it comes to a pitcher's mechanics, discretion is the better part of valor.

Runners on First and Second

Again, you should get the force out at second and hope for the double play. The pitcher to shortstop to first (1-6-3) double play is much easier to turn than throwing the ball to the third baseman, because he has to throw the ball all the way across the diamond. You should throw to third base only on a slowly hit ball to the third-base side of the mound, or if you bobble the ball and have no time to get a double play. Go to first base only on a slowly hit ball to the right side of the mound (to your left). Listen for instructions from your catcher as you field the ball. He can see everything developing directly in front of him.

Runners on First and Third

Unless the runner on third represents the tying or go-ahead run and it's late in the game, you should throw the ball to second base to attempt the double play. If the runner at third represents the tying or winning run, you should check him back to the base before throwing the ball to second. (If he breaks for home, throw the ball to the catcher.) This is the most complicated defensive situation you'll face. You should frequently practice defending against the first-and-third situation.

Bases Loaded

At higher levels of baseball, coaches prefer that the pitcher throw the ball to second base in this situation. For Little League players though, I believe the pitcher should initiate the double play by throwing the ball to the catcher. Throw the ball chest-high and out over the plate, leading the catcher into fair territory. Make sure of your throw, because you want to cut off the run. If the ball is slowly hit you may still have time to get the force-out at the plate. Always look for an opportunity to stop a run from scoring.

Runner on Second and/or Third

The force play is not available. You must prethink how you will handle this situation. As soon as you field the ball you must check the position of the runner. If he breaks for the next base, throw him out. If you catch him halfway between the bases you should run directly at him, forcing him to run one way or the other. Once he commits to a base you should throw the ball to your fielder, then follow the throw and be prepared to be involved in a rundown play. If the runner heads back to his original base simply throw the ball to first base and take the easy out.

Ground Ball to the Right Side of the Infield

On any ground ball hit to the right side of the infield, between first and second base, the pitcher automatically breaks toward first base, preparing to cover the base if needed. This is a play that is practiced over and over in preseason and during the season. As soon as the ball is hit, the catcher and all the players in the dugout should shout at the pitcher to "get over!" Here are the steps to follow for covering first base:

1. React immediately toward first base, no matter how routine the ground ball may seem (first basemen have been known to bobble routine grounders).
2. Sprint toward the foul line to a spot about 10 feet short of the base.
3. Slow down and come under control as you reach the foul line.
4. Present a target with your glove and ask for the ball.
5. Catch the ball first, and then look for the base.
6. Touch the inside of the base with your right foot and allow your momentum to carry you in toward fair territory (touch-

As soon as a ground ball is hit to the right side of the infield, the pitcher breaks toward first base.

If the first baseman can't get the out himself, he delivers an underhand toss to the pitcher covering first base.

The pitcher catches the ball and touches the inside of the base with his right foot. He should then turn immediately toward the infield to check the position of any base runners.

ing the base with your left foot or crossing the foul line may get you barreled over by the runner).

7. Turn back toward the infield to check the position of any base runners.

If the pitcher gets to the base before receiving the throw, he should set up like a first baseman, contacting the inside of the base with the right foot. Any time the first baseman waves the pitcher away from the bag, the pitcher should yield and allow him to take the ball to the base himself.

Fielding Bunts

Bunting is very popular among Little League hitters. It's very important that pitchers know their responsibilities for defending against the bunt. They should anticipate the bunt and know what to do with the ball once it's fielded. Assume you're the pitcher as these bunt scenarios are discussed.

Bases Empty

Get to the ball as quickly as possible. If the ball is still rolling use your glove. If the ball has come to rest use your bare hand. Use quick footwork to square your shoulders to first base and use your quickest release by taking a limited backswing. Don't worry too much about the velocity of your throw. A quick, accurate throw is much more important. Also, don't rush your throw, because you probably have more time than you think.

Runner on First

Unless the ball is bunted hard and right at you, your best play will be to first base. Get the sure out. A hitter who is attempting a sacrifice bunt is offering you an out. Take it!

On a ball bunted back to the mound, the pitcher calls for and fields the ball. He squares his feet and throws to the first-base bag.

The pitcher never throws the ball directly to the second baseman if he's approaching the base, but rather leads him to the base with his throw.

Runners on First and Second

Again, unless the ball is bunted hard to you, your best play is probably to first base. If you are a right-handed pitcher and want to make the play at third base you should execute a reverse pivot before throwing. That is, you should field the ball, step away from third base with your right foot, turn your left shoulder and left foot toward third base, and throw the ball.

Squeeze Play

With a runner on third base, less than two outs, and no force play available at the plate, you should be ready for the "squeeze play," a sacrifice bunt designed to drive home a run. If the play is well disguised you probably won't have a chance to get the runner at home. Simply throw the ball to first base and get the out. If, however, the batter prematurely squares to bunt, you should pitch the ball high and away from the batter, to make it difficult for him to bunt.

Pop-Ups

In professional baseball the pitcher rarely fields a pop-up. That's partly because he is surrounded by a complement of outstanding fielders. In Little League baseball the pitcher is often the best athlete on the field, so he should field any pop-up he can easily catch. The pitcher should call for the ball loudly and clearly: "I got it. I got it." When the pitcher can't field the ball, he should bark out instructions as to who should catch the ball: "Tommy! Tommy! Tommy!" Then, he should cover the base left vacant by the fielder who is fielding the pop-up. On pop-ups behind the catcher, the pitcher should point to the ball and shout instructions to the catcher: "Straight back!"

HOLD PROGRAM

Little League pitchers don't need to hold runners on base, because there's no leading allowed while the pitcher is holding the ball. Still, it won't be long before they are charged with the responsibility of holding runners close, so now is not a bad time to start learning the crucial elements of the Hold Program, a system for keeping runners from stealing you blind.

There are many reasons for keeping base runners honest:

- It keeps the double play in order.
- Runners are kept out of scoring position.
- Your catcher gets a chance to throw out base stealers.
- The other team has to get more hits to score runs.
- It takes pressure off your defense.

The Hold Program is comprised of several simple and logical concepts. Pitchers' skill at holding runners close is a product of their commitment. If they accept their responsibility for holding runners, they'll be good at it. If they don't, they won't. Here is a checklist of techniques you should incorporate into your Hold Program:

- ☐ Vary the length of time that the pitcher holds the ball in the set position. This makes it difficult for the runner to time his move to the plate.
- ☐ Pitchers should learn and use a slide-step delivery. This is an abbreviated delivery, without the normal leg raise that allows them to deliver the ball to the catcher more quickly.
- ☐ Perfect the pickoff move to first. A quick and/or deceptive move will force the base runner to take a shorter primary lead, meaning that he'll have to run farther to steal a base.

☐ Hold the ball. Nothing destroys the rhythm and timing of a base stealer more than a pitcher who holds the ball for long periods of time. The runner will be flat-footed and tense, and he may even break for second before the ball is released, thus giving you an easy out.

Backing Up Bases

Inevitably there will be balls hit to the outfield with runners on base. When this happens the pitcher can't just stand there like a statue, lamenting the location of the pitch or the poor pursuit angle taken by the right fielder. I've seen too many pitchers get

On plays at third base and/or home plate, the pitcher hustles to back up the throw. The pitcher must remember to give himself enough distance behind the base to react to an errant throw. If he sets up too close, the ball will likely skip past him.

caught up in the moment, standing behind the mound with their hands on their hips when they should be getting into better position to help their defense. Like it or not, backing up bases is a crucial part of a pitcher's job. Make sure the pitcher keeps these points in mind:

- Never stand still. There is a place for you to be after every ball hit to the outfield. Get there as quickly as possible.
- Watch the runners as they move around the bases and react to where the ball is going. On a base hit to the outfield you should head for the base that is two bases ahead of the lead runner.
- When you back up a base stand as far back from the base as the field layout allows. This gives you time to react to an off-line throw. Also, try to place yourself in a direct line with the base and the position of the fielder who is throwing the ball.
- Expect the unexpected. Be prepared for a good throw to be mishandled or to carom off the runner.
- If you catch an overthrow be prepared to make a play.

70

On a ball hit to the outfield fence with no runners on base, the pitcher should immediately back up third. He should concede that any ball hit that far is at least a double and go to the next base.

> *There is always a spot for the pitcher to be. He should never be standing on the mound watching the game go by. The pitcher should always be anticipating where an overthrow might be and pay attention to what the base runners are doing.*
>
> *—Jim Kaat, major-league pitcher (16-time Gold Glove winner)*

Fielding Drills

Here are some of the most common fielding drills for pitchers. They all come under the broad heading of Pitcher's Fielding Practice, or PFP.

Comebackers

This is a simple drill where the pitcher simulates the delivery of a pitch, then fields a ground ball hit to him by the coach. The pitcher fields the ball and throws to a designated base. You can make the drill more fun by playing a game called "Knockout." In Knockout, the pitcher must field the ball cleanly and make an accurate throw or he is out of the game. The last pitcher in the game is the winner.

Bunts

Combine bunting practice for the hitters with bunt fielding practice for the pitchers. Wait until the pitcher nearly reaches the ball before calling out a designated base for him to throw to. You may more closely simulate game conditions by not allowing the pitcher to break for the ball until he hears a verbal signal from a coach.

Rundowns

Simulate a rundown between third base and home. The pitcher begins with the ball at home plate and the runner halfway up the baseline. Create a game in which two-man teams (pitcher and infielder) compete to retire the runner with the least number of throws possible. Each team gets four or five attempts, with a point awarded for each time they record an out with only one throw, and a point subtracted for each time they allow the runner to be safe.

Covering First

The pitcher simulates a pitch, the coach hits a ground ball to the right side of the infield, and the pitcher covers first. Repeat 10 times for each pitcher.

6

THE CATCHER

In football, the "field general" is a term used for the quarterback. On the baseball field, that title belongs to the catcher. The masked man behind home plate is the leader of the defensive unit. Good catchers possess strong skills in two separate areas. The first area is physical talent. Gone are the days of the big, slow catcher. Coaches had traditionally placed a player of size behind home plate. While a big catcher may give pitchers psychological comfort by offering a broad target, there are several aspects of catching where a sluggish catcher can fall short.

Excellent defensive catchers are agile and have soft hands and quick feet. There is much more to catching than offering a big target. Blocking balls, framing, popping out of the catcher's stance on steal attempts, and fielding bunts all require quickness and athleticism. Today's prototypical catcher is physically strong, but he's also often the best athlete on the team.

The second skill area of good catchers is leadership. Quality catchers are good communicators, authoritative, decisive, controlling, and supportive. They call out bases for balls to be thrown, align cutoff men, relay signs, and exercise methods to calm or spark the pitching staff. A good catcher should have a noticeable presence on the baseball field.

> *A good catcher is the quarterback, the carburetor, the lead dog,*
> *the pulse taker, the traffic cop, and sometimes a lot of unprintable*
> *things, but no team gets very far without one.*
> —Miller Huggins, former major-league manager

The Catcher's Stance

To assume a basic catcher's stance, the catcher squats down and positions his feet slightly farther than shoulder-width apart. The feet are splayed a bit outward, with his weight on the inside of his ankles. There is a slight forward lean with the upper body, and the throwing hand is held behind the right heel. The left elbow rests above the left knee, and the glove is held out for a target. The fingers of the catcher's mitt should point toward the pitcher, and the pocket is held open facing the ground. This helps emphasize a low target to the pitcher.

With runners on base, the catcher raises his tail end slightly. This puts him in a more agile position to race out on bunt plays and to shift his feet to throw on steal attempts.

Receiving

A good receiver at home plate makes the pitcher better. Pitchers feel greater comfort when throwing the ball at maximum velocity if they're not nervous about their pitches being mishandled by the catcher. Also, the catcher can make pitches look better by "framing" the pitches. Turning borderline pitches into called strikes can have a major impact on a game.

The best catchers take pride in how they receive pitches. Again, good catching gives pitchers a sense of comfort, and it gives a good

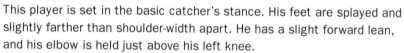

This player is set in the basic catcher's stance. His feet are splayed and slightly farther than shoulder-width apart. He has a slight forward lean, and his elbow is held just above his left knee.

presentation to the umpire. It's not enough to simply catch the ball from the pitcher. The catcher should receive the ball as if practicing an art form.

Framing

Umpires want to call strikes. It's in their nature. Strikes keep the game alive and moving. Calling ball after ball reduces the flow of a game to a snail's pace. With this in mind, catchers should make a concerted effort to make every pitch look as good as possible. Give the umpire any reason or opportunity to raise his arm and call, "Strike!"

Pitches that require framing are ones that are on the border or just outside of the strike zone. Catchers should not frame pitches within the heart of the strike zone. The umpire may feel insulted by the catcher attempting to sell a pitch that is obviously a strike. It is also important that catchers do not attempt to frame pitches that are well out of the strike zone. This also can be construed as "demeaning" to the umpire and should not be practiced by the catcher. Good catchers frame pitches that need framing. Anything outside of that and the craft begins to lose it effectiveness.

When framing pitches, the catcher should keep one thought in mind: less is more. The less body movement used to frame the pitch, the more strikes will be called. Most of the framing work is performed by the glove hand and wrist. The body can shift slightly before receiving the ball to give the umpire a better look, but any exaggerated movements reduce the chance of getting a called strike.

On pitches that are borderline high, outside, or inside, teach the catcher to glove the outside of the ball (the portion of the ball outside the strike zone). For example, let's say there is a right-handed batter at the plate and the pitch is just off the outside corner. The catcher prepares his glove to corral the right side of the ball. As the ball is received, he turns his hand and wrist in toward the strike zone.

The catcher uses the same approach on an inside pitch. Receive the outside of the ball and turn the hand and wrist in toward the strike zone. High strikes require the catcher to receive the top of the ball and turn the glove down. Make sure the movement is subtle and made only with the hand and wrist. Pulling the glove down with the entire arm is a bad sell and an obvious frame in the eyes of the umpire.

The low strike is the most difficult pitch to frame. As the pitch approaches home plate, the catcher quarter-turns his glove down and attempts to catch just the top half of the ball. The ball is caught down near the web (not the pocket) so it gives the appearance that the glove did not have to dive down too far to frame the pitch. Pull the glove up ever so slightly, but again, yanking it up ruins the chance of a sell to the ump.

Framing the ball improves the presentation of the pitch. This pitch is slightly off the plate, but turning the glove inward toward home plate increases the chance of a called strike.

Low pitches are the most difficult to frame. Here, the catcher quarter-turns his glove down and catches the top of the ball with the web of the glove.

Blocking

A catcher who blocks pitches in the dirt is invaluable to a Little League team. Young pitchers have yet to develop consistent command of their pitches and because pitchers are taught to aim low, the majority of their errant throws are in the dirt. Catchers who are able to block the ball hold base runners at bay. Runners are unable to advance or, more important, to score on balls in the dirt.

The initial phase of blocking pitches is recognition. Catchers must learn to quickly recognize when a ball is destined to hit the ground before they can catch it. The sooner they determine this, the sooner they can leave their catcher's stance and get into position to block the pitch. This is an acquired skill that is developed through repetition. A good exercise to improve recognition is to throw pitch after pitch to a catcher, alternating between balls that reach and balls in the dirt. To keep the catcher from getting beat up, use tennis balls during this drill.

After a catcher recognizes that the pitch is destined for the dirt, he assumes an aggressive attitude. He must attack the ball to block it, rather than allowing the ball to attack him. From the stance position, the catcher immediately falls forward to his knees. The glove and hand drop down in front of him. The catcher leans forward with his upper body, rounds his shoulders inward, and tucks his chin to his chest. The object is to keep the ball in front so every part of the body is positioned to redirect the ball down and in front. The elbows are also kept close to the body to prevent balls from slipping between the arms.

Once the catcher recognizes the pitch will bounce in the dirt, he drops to his knees to block the pitch.

The catcher must always keep in mind that the object is to block the ball. He should not try to catch it or he will spring holes in any attempt to do so. Another good piece of advice is to teach the catcher to block the ball from the direction it came from. This gets him behind the ball and if he keeps it in front, runners will be unable to advance.

Balls that are wild low and to the side are more difficult to handle. The catcher has to do his best to get his body in front of the ball. As he falls forward, he shifts his body in the direction of the pitch. On balls extremely wide of the strike zone, the catcher takes a quick jab step in the direction of the pitch before shifting and dropping to his knees. This enables him to increase his range blocking pitches.

On pitches that are wild low and to the side, the catcher shifts his body as he drops down in an attempt to get his body in front of the pitch.

Defending the Steal

A strong arm is an asset behind home plate, but only if the catcher is able to get rid of the ball in a timely fashion. To defend the steal consistently, a catcher must have quick feet and a quick release. A strong arm is a bonus.

In a potential steal situation, the catcher raises his rear end in his stance. This places him in a better position to deliver a quick, strong throw. After adjusting his stance slightly, the catcher may employ one of three methods of footwork when attempting to throw out a runner stealing second base. It's the job of the catcher and coach to determine which method works best.

Jump Pivot Method

The jump pivot is the method most commonly used by catchers. A catcher must have quick and agile feet to employ this technique. As the ball is received, the catcher quickly shifts his feet. The shoulders align with second base, and the right foot shifts clockwise so that it points toward the first-base dugout. The catcher transfers his weight forward and takes a short jab step with his left foot toward second base.

Rocker Step Method

For catchers possessing above-average arms, there is the rocker step method. As the ball is received, the catcher rocks back on his right foot, squares his shoulders, takes a short step with the left foot, and throws. This technique offers the quickest release, but a catcher must have excellent arm strength to cut down the runner.

The jump pivot method. As the ball is received, the catcher shifts his feet, takes a short jab step with the left foot, and fires to second base.

The rocker step method. As the ball is received, the catcher rocks back on his right leg, squares his shoulders to second base, takes a short jab step, and fires to second base.

Throw to Third Base

The throw to third base on a steal attempt is a shorter throw. Footwork and quickness are essential in throwing the runner out. Often, the location of the pitch dictates where the catcher takes his steps. Also a factor is where the hitter stands in the batter's box.

On pitches down the middle, the catcher can step forward with the right foot to move in front of the batter (now to his left). He then squares his shoulders to third base, steps with the left foot, and throws to third base. This path can also be taken on outside pitches to a right-handed hitter. On inside strikes to a right-handed batter, the catcher takes a short step back with his right foot, squares his shoulders, takes a step toward third base with the left foot, and throws behind the batter. With a left-handed hitter at the plate, the catcher can simply take a jab step with his left foot, square his shoulders, and fire to third base.

Throwing Form

To release the ball quickly, a catcher must shorten his backswing. Dropping the arm down, back, and up simply takes too long. As the ball is taken from the catcher's mitt, the throwing arm is drawn straight back (about shoulder level). A catcher's throw on a steal attempt should be more like a middle infielder's than like an outfielder's or a pitcher's.

Fielding Bunts

An offense usually executes a sacrifice bunt during a critical point in the game. Whether it's to move a runner into scoring position to tie a game, take a lead, or cushion a lead, the offense sacrifices an out to advance a runner. It's imperative that the defense capitalize on that "sacrificed" out. If an offense is giving up an out, the defense has got to take it.

The catcher plays a significant role on sacrifice bunt plays. If he is not fielding the ball, he is directing his teammate where to throw the ball. "One! One! One!" means first base. "Two! Two! Two!" means the throw goes to second base. The catcher must be loud and clear with his calls.

On short bunts, the catcher must pop out from behind home plate and make the play himself. He should immediately take off his mask, toss it to the side, and trail the ball. A catcher who hustles can often get the lead runner on bunts.

Fielding the Ball

When fielding the bunt, the catcher scoops the ball into his mitt. To do this, the throwing hand and glove are held on opposite sides of the ball. The catcher brings his hands together by scooping the ball with his bare hand into the mitt. The catcher should never attempt to field a rolling bunt with only his glove or just his bare hand. He should use two hands.

The catcher should use his bare hand to pick up the ball only if it has stopped rolling completely. In this case, the catcher grabs the top of the ball with his bare hand, pushes it into the ground, and then picks it up. Pushing the ball into the ground ensures a firm grip.

Bunts to First Base

The catcher must be deliberate with his footwork to make sure he's lined up to first base and in a balanced position to make the throw. On bunts to first base, the catcher takes a quick shuffle step after fielding the ball and makes a strong throw to the inside of the base. If the ball is right down the first-base line, the catcher takes a step back toward the infield with his right foot. He then steps toward first base with his left foot and throws. Taking a step back toward

To scoop the ball, the catcher runs to the left side of the ball and aligns his feet with first base.

He separates his throwing hand from his glove and then brings them together to securely field the ball.

the infield provides the catcher a throwing lane. Failing to take that step runs the risk of hitting the runner with the throw.

Bunts to Third Base

On bunts down the third-base line, the catcher runs to the infield side of the ball. He scoops the ball and plants heavily on his right leg. The catcher turns his shoulders to align with first base, steps, and throws. Running to the left of the ball should be done only when the ball is bunted toward the shortstop position. In this case, the catcher scoops the ball, quickly squares his feet to first base, and throws.

Catcher Pop-Ups

One of the toughest plays on the baseball field is the catcher pop-up. The catcher has to first find the ball, shed gear, factor in the backspin on the ball, and catch a fly ball with a catcher's mitt. It's not an easy play, but catchers get much better at making the play when they know the proper steps to take.

When the ball goes up, the catcher must immediately rise from his crouch, turn his back to the infield, and remove his mask. Once the catcher locates the ball, he runs over to it and tosses his mask far off to the side. The mask should not be tossed until the ball is found. Should the catcher toss the mask before he finds the ball, he may eventually trip over it.

On catcher pop-ups, the catcher finds the ball first while holding his mask.

Once he locates the ball and runs under it, he tosses his mask to the side and out of harm's way.

Balls that are popped up behind home plate have tremendous backspin. The barrel of the bat clips the very bottom of the ball, causing it to ascend straight up in the air. Because there is backspin, the ball will fall toward the infield. It will not drop straight down. The catcher must factor this in when positioning himself to make the catch. If he finds the ball and gets directly under it, he should take two steps back toward the infield to account for the backspin's influence on the ball's descent.

The ball is caught with two hands. If anyone is on base, the catcher immediately turns toward the infield in case a base runner attempts to tag up. The pitcher always covers home plate with a runner on third and less than two outs.

The catch is made with two hands, back turned to the infield.

Catcher Pop-Ups: Five Steps, One Out

The catcher should

1. Stand up, remove his mask, and turn his back to the field.
2. Locate the ball and run over to the area of its descent.
3. Toss the mask far to the side.
4. Get under the ball and take two steps back toward the infield to give consideration to the backspin.
5. Catch the ball with two hands.

87

Using tennis balls during the Block or Frame drill allows the catcher to focus on form without the fear of getting hurt.

Drills

Block or Frame

Using tennis balls or IncrediBalls, a coach throws pitches from the front of the pitcher's mound. He throws some pitches that reach the catcher and others that are in the dirt. When a pitch reaches the catcher the catcher practices framing the pitch to make it look like a strike. On balls in the dirt, the catcher works on blocking the ball and keeping in front. The location of the pitches should vary as well.

By getting both pitches in the dirt and balls that reach him, the catcher improves his reaction time in knowing when to drop to his knees (block) and when to stay up and receive the pitch (frame).

Quick Feet

Proper footwork is so important to a catcher making a quick, accurate throw to second and third base on steal plays. It's something that isn't practiced enough because the focus is always on the throw itself.

In this drill, the catcher works on his footwork only. From the squat position, the catcher receives the pitch and quickly pops up into throwing position. He should use one of the three pivot methods or experiment with new techniques to see what works best. The quicker the release, the fewer steps the base runner has taken before the ball is thrown.

Bunt Feeds

A coach stands behind the catcher who is in the squat position. The coach rolls the ball out toward first base, third base, and directly out in front and calls out the destination of each throw. The catcher fields the ball, squares his feet and shoulders, makes sure he has a clear throwing lane, and throws.

This is a drill that cannot be practiced enough. It's a play that must be executed without thought in a game. Sacrifice bunts come at critical times in the game, so it's essential that the defense secure an out.

7

THE FIRST BASEMAN

There are times in a Little League baseball game when it feels like all the stars in the sky must be aligned to record a ground ball out in the infield. Frankly, there are several steps that must be properly executed without making a mistake for that to happen. Players must be in position and prepared for a ball to be hit to them. The pitcher must throw a pitch that induces the hitter to swing and produce a ground ball. The infielder must glove the ball and throw it to first base in time to beat the runner.

It would be nice to think that at this point, the play is over. Put an out up on the scoreboard and throw the ball around the horn. But that's not the case. A task that is often overlooked still needs to take place before the umpire raises his fist to the air. The first baseman must make a clean catch while holding the first-base bag to complete the play.

The importance of the first baseman must not be underestimated. As David Falkner writes in his book *Nine Sides of the Diamond*, "From the moment it was decided that putouts were to be recorded by means of a throw to first base, securely held by a fielder, first basemen have been guaranteed more action in the course of a game than all other position players save the pitcher and catcher." A

Great defensive plays in the infield require the first baseman to squeeze the ball in his glove to complete the out.

good first baseman solidifies an infield's defense. A great first baseman makes his entire infield defense better. His ability to receive throws accurate or errant instills confidence in the minds of infielders, enabling them to play relaxed and aggressively.

When infielders are confident their first baseman will catch any throw within reach, their accuracy improves. They don't concern themselves with being so precise that they tense up and "aim" or "guide" their throw to first base. The infielder is able to stay athletic and deliver the ball with assurance. In addition, infielders will feel as if they have the option to "gun" a throw to first if necessary. Balls that are bobbled or hit in the hole often require the infielder to put something extra on the throw to have a chance at the runner. Having a sure-handed first baseman allows infielders to unleash throws they might otherwise hold onto.

A first baseman doesn't necessarily have to be a big player, but it certainly doesn't hurt. A taller player will reach throws (while holding the bag) that a shorter player will have to leave the ground to catch. Taller players generally have longer legs, enabling them to stretch farther forward and to the side. They typically have longer arms, which also increases their vertical and lateral range while holding the base. And psychologically, infielders feel comfortable throwing to a bigger target, provided they can catch. There are first basemen on the shorter side who are outstanding at their position. But you can't teach size.

Positioning

Certain game situations will dictate adjustments in positioning at first base, but for now, we'll discuss where a Little League first baseman positions himself with nobody on and nobody out. When playing at regular depth, a Little League first baseman must be aware of two main factors when positioning himself in the field. How fast am I, and how fast is the runner at home plate? By combining those two factors, the first baseman can establish an educated guess as to how far he can play from the base and comfortably beat the batter to first on a ground ball.

The most common positioning mistake first basemen are guilty of is that they play too close to the base. They are so scared they won't get to the base in time to receive a throw from an infielder that they "hug" the base. This decreases their range in the infield. Balls they might be able to field by playing deeper or farther off the bag, instead pass through the infield for a clean base hit.

Here is a simple, but worthy tip to give first basemen. As soon as a ground ball is hit—whether it be to the second baseman, third baseman, shortstop—find the first base with your eyes and immediately sprint to it. Do not become a spectator and watch your teammate field the ball. Get to the base *first*! Often first basemen never take their eyes off the play, coast toward the base, and then search for the bag with their feet. This is not time-effective and could prove costly. They should get to the base, position themselves, and then look to the player delivering the throw.

As soon as the ball leaves the bat, the first baseman moves quickly to first base to set his feet.

At regular depth, the first baseman should be positioned four or five steps behind the base and three or four steps to the right of the bag. The more territory a first baseman is able to cover on the right side of the infield, the more the second baseman can cheat toward second base.

Positioning should change with each hitter. For example, when defending a fleet-footed, left-handed hitter, the first baseman may have to play a little closer to the bag. If a big, hard-hitting lefty batter is at the plate, the first baseman might play deeper. Against a right-handed hitter, the first baseman can cheat more toward second base.

Here are specific game situations and how first basemen might want to adjust their positioning in each:

- *Bunt situation:* up on the grass
- *Double-play depth:* just in front of or just behind the bag, three or four steps to the right of the base
- *Bases loaded, less than two outs:* up on the grass, two or three steps to the right of the base
- *One run ahead or tie score, late in the game, nobody on:* deep and toward the first-base line

Receiving the Throw

After the first baseman hustles over to first base on a ground ball, he positions both heels on the corner of the base and squares his upper body to his teammate delivering the throw. From here, the first baseman *waits* to see the flight of the throw. This is critical. Too often first basemen get into the stretch position before seeing the throw. This works okay if the throw is accurate, but it restricts their range if the throw is inaccurate.

If the throw is on target, the first baseman steps toward the throw (right-handed players with their left foot; left-handed players with their right foot) and reaches for the ball with the glove. For a right-handed first baseman on a throw that is off-line to the left, the right heel moves to the infield-side corner of the base, and the left foot and glove stretch out to receive the ball. On throws off-line to the right, the right heel moves to the outfield-side corner of the bag, and the left foot and glove stretch out for the throw. For left-handers, the left heel is placed on the corner of the bag and the right leg stretches for the throw.

Another reason first basemen should refrain from stretching too early is fielding errant throws that are wild high. By stretching prematurely, the first baseman has just made himself a shorter target.

The first baseman squares up to his teammate delivering the throw. He does NOT stretch for the throw until he sees the flight of the ball. Once he sees the throw, he steps to the ball with his glove-side foot.

By waiting to see the flight of the ball, the first baseman increases his range dramatically. Here, the throw was wide to the first baseman's left and he was able to step in that direction to hold the bag and make the catch.

He may not be able to reach a throw that sails high. He'll also be unable to jump up for throws from the stretch position.

Stretching for the ball is important. Simply put, it allows the first baseman to receive the ball earlier. On close plays, the first baseman's stretch can be the deciding factor in whether or not a runner is called out. Also, stretching can enable the first baseman to catch a short throw in the air rather than having to pick it out of the dirt.

Balls in the Dirt

Picking balls out of the dirt is a tough play for a first baseman, but if it becomes a strength he'll be loved by his infielders. The first step in successfully catching balls out of the dirt is judgment. The first baseman must quickly measure the distance of the throw. If he can catch the ball on the short hop, the first baseman stretches and

Whoever says this is an easy position doesn't know what he's talking about. Just getting your hands and feet to work right together is tough enough.

—Dwight Evans, former Boston Red Sox all-star right fielder who played 64 games at first base in 1988

attempts to scoop the ball. If it's too far short to pick, the first baseman should stay back and play the long hop. The only way to improve judgment is to practice seeing balls in the dirt thrown from the infield positions. By seeing ball after ball, the first baseman will not only make better decisions but will make them sooner.

The first baseman lowers his glove and scoops forward when picking a ball out of the dirt. His head (and eyes) must remain down and follow the ball as long as possible.

To scoop the ball, the first baseman stretches and reaches out with the glove. Whether it's to the glove side or backhand, the glove is held low just above the ground. To make the scoop, the glove is moved forward through the ball. This is an athletic play, so the glove hand must stay tension-free to be effective. Attempt to receive the ball in the glove's web, and field through the ball with one hand.

97

When playing the long hop, the first baseman stays back at the base and bends down at the knees. This lowers the eyes closer to the ball and improves the read. If the hop is long enough, the first baseman can reach for the ball with his glove. If it's more of an in-between hop, he should stay back and give with his glove, seeing the ball as long as possible.

On a long hop, the first baseman stays back to receive the ball. He waits for the ball to bounce up and catches the ball with two hands.

Throws to Second Base

With a runner on first base and less than two outs, the double play is in order. The first baseman is going to play in front of the base (and runner) or behind the base (and runner) depending on the batter and game situation. The most important aspect of making a throw to second after fielding a ground ball is to square the feet and shoulders to second base before making the throw.

For left-handed first basemen, this is a much easier play. Their feet are typically squared up with second base upon fielding the baseball. Left-handers must simply make sure they have a clear throwing lane and step and throw to the target.

Right-handed first basemen must shift their feet after fielding the ball. On balls hit at them or to their right, they turn to the right by dropping the right foot back, then step with the left foot to square the feet and shoulders to the target, and throw. On balls that take them to their left (toward the first-base line) or forward, they should use a reverse pivot. To execute a reverse pivot, they turn left by taking a crossover step with their right foot (right over left). As they plant with their right foot, the shoulders turn left and align themselves with the target, they take a short jab with the left foot to the target, and fire to second base.

In the event the first baseman is playing up in front of the base, he's going to throw to the inside of second base after fielding the ball. That means the shortstop sets up to the infield side of second base to receive the throw. This gives the first baseman a clear path to throw the ball. By wrongly setting up to the outfield side of the base, the shortstop is forcing the first baseman to throw across the base path and risk hitting the runner with the throw.

If the first baseman is playing behind the base, he'll throw to the outside of second base. The shortstop sets up to the outfield side of second base to give the first baseman a clear throwing lane.

On balls hit near the first-base bag, the first baseman should retreat back to the bag to receive the throw from the shortstop. If

When the first baseman fields the ball up near the grass, he throws to the inside of second base on a force play.

If he is positioned deep, the first baseman throws to the outside of second base on a force play.

the ball takes him far away from the base, the pitcher should be running over on contact and should take the throw at first. Keep the second baseman out of there!

Bunt Plays

In a sacrifice bunt situation, the first baseman plays up on the grass. When the hitter squares or pivots showing bunt, he gains ground and moves in toward home plate. If the ball is bunted in his area, the first baseman must do two things: (1) field the ball cleanly; (2) listen to direction from the catcher. The catcher is the commander on bunt plays, so if he yells, "One! One! One!" the first baseman squares his feet with and throws to first base (covered by the second baseman). If the catcher calls out, "Two! Two! Two!" the first baseman squares his feet with and throws to second base (covered by the shortstop). The most important aspect of defending the bunt is that you get an out. If you have a good shot at the lead runner, get him. But if it's too risky, get the out at first base.

How an Offense Might Tip the Bunt

- Third-base coach calls extra attention to himself and goes through a sequence of signs.
- Batter moves up in the box.
- Batter moves closer to home plate.
- Base runner seems more attentive and intense on the base.
- Batter chokes up or demonstrates something different in his stance position.
- Players in dugout become more alert, whisper to each other, or become dead quiet.

Relay Throws

On all throws from center and right field to home plate, the first baseman immediately shifts into position to provide a cutoff for the outfielder. With an opposing runner on second base, for example, the first baseman becomes the cutoff man on a base hit to right field. The precise positioning is a combined effort between the catcher and first baseman. The catcher aligns the first baseman (who is facing the outfielder) between the outfielder and home plate. The first baseman listens to the call of the catcher and adjusts accordingly. If the catcher yells, "Left! Left! Left!" the first baseman shuffles to the left until the catcher ceases directing. If the catcher yells, "Right! Right! Right!" the first baseman shuffles to the right.

The depth of positioning depends on two factors: how shallow or deep the outfielder gloves the ball, and the strength of his arm. It's essential that the first baseman is aware of how well his teammate throws. Move farther out if the outfielder has a weak arm, and drop back deeper if he has a strong arm.

On balls hit to center field, the first baseman sprints to the back of the pitcher's mound. He should not watch the play! This results in coasting to the spot, and he may not get set in time. Teach the first baseman to set his eyesight to the back of the mound and sprint there.

As the first baseman sets up for the throw, he holds his arms up in the air for the outfielder. He does not square up exactly and face the outfielder. Instead, teach him to drop his glove-side foot back and open his body up slightly toward the glove side. Instruct him to make every effort to catch the ball on his glove side. This saves time when relaying the throw to home plate.

Once the ball is in flight, the first baseman again listens to the direction of the catcher. If the catcher says nothing, it's the first

On throws home from right field, the first baseman serves as the cutoff man. He raises his arms and sets up slightly open to make the catch and throw a quicker transition.

baseman's responsibility to let the ball go. He should not touch it! It means the throw is a good one and on path to cutting down the runner at the plate. If the ball is to be intercepted, the catcher will yell, "Cut!" The command, "Cut four!" means cut the ball off and immediately throw home. The command, "Cut two!" means cut the ball off and immediately throw to second base. The ball is always received with two hands. This assists in transferring the ball from the glove to the throwing hand.

Not every ball will be thrown perfectly. Some throws will be short, long, left, or right. The first baseman must quickly respond to errant throws by adjusting his position when he notices that the ball in flight is off-line. He does not have to hold his line. If the throw is off-line to his right, the first baseman moves to the right as the ball is in flight and forces the ball to his glove side. On balls thrown short, the first baseman moves up to try to catch the ball before it hits the ground, and on deep throws the player drops back. The primary objective is to catch every ball in the air. The second objective is to catch on the glove side. The cutoff man stays active in his attempts to achieve his objectives.

Drills

Around the Horn

First basemen are known as receivers, but they're also responsible for delivering important throws in a game. This often gets over-looked. To run this drill, a coach stands at home plate hitting ground balls, while players are positioned at third base, second base, home plate, and the pitcher's mound. The first baseman positions himself up on the infield grass.

The coach hits a ground ball that the first baseman fields and throws to third base. The first baseman retreats to first base, finds the bag, and receives a return throw from the third baseman. The second ground ball is fielded by the first baseman and thrown to second base. He retreats to first base to receive the return throw. The first baseman then plays deep, fields a ground ball, and delivers an underhand toss to the pitcher covering. The first baseman then creeps back up to the infield grass, fields a ground ball, and fires home to the catcher. The first baseman practices fielding ground balls, throwing, finding the base, and receiving throws in this drill. It's an important position, and each aspect of playing it should be given its due attention.

First-Base Cleanup

A good first baseman is like a vacuum. He sucks up everything within his reach. With the first baseman positioned at the first-base bag, a coach delivers errant throws from second base, shortstop, and third base.

The first baseman must initially focus on reading the throw. It is only then that he should decide whether to stretch, reach up, step right, left, or leave the bag. This drill is designed to develop judgment as much as to improve receiving skills. The coach should throw balls in the dirt, high, and wide. He should also throw balls from different arm angles, giving the ball different carry and spins in the dirt.

8

THE THIRD BASEMAN

While the middle infield positions of shortstop and second base often receive the most attention in a Little League infield, the third baseman is extremely important on several different levels. A quality third baseman increases the shortstop's range, guns down runners at the plate on relays from left field, can shut down the opposition's bunting game, and completes outs on tag plays. A standout third baseman helps make the left side of the infield, where most ground balls are hit in Little League baseball, airtight.

There are obvious skills third basemen should have to excel at their position. They must be adept at fielding ground balls, possess a strong throwing arm, and showcase quickness and agility. But there are additional characteristics that extend beyond fielding skills. A good third baseman is instinctual, aggressive, and fearless. Because third basemen man the position nearest the hitter, a batted ball gets on them rapidly, so their initial reaction has to be the correct one to make plays consistently.

"I have never been afraid ever of taking a ground ball in the face," said former Cardinals third baseman Terry Pendleton, "because I've always known that I could get my head out of the way in time. The head is actually the first part of the body that moves. People may not

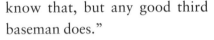

The third baseman is set in the ready position. Being in good position on every pitch enables the third baseman to react quickly.

know that, but any good third baseman does."

There are two points a third baseman should keep in mind on the field. First, he should attempt to field anything he can reach. On ground balls to the left, he should make every effort to field the ball in front of the shortstop. In doing so, the third baseman gloves the ball sooner, has a shorter throw, and has the momentum going toward first base. The same philosophy applies when a slow roller is hit to the left of the pitcher's mound. The third baseman should make that play whenever possible.

The second point is that when a hard-hit ball is hit directly at him, the third baseman should understand that he has time. The ball gets to him as the hitter is just leaving the batter's box. It's not even necessary to field the ball clean. The third baseman should stay in front of the ball to make sure he at least knocks it down, square his feet, and make the throw to first. He should never panic.

Positioning

Third basemen adjust their position on the field for nearly every batter. At times, they'll even adjust from pitch to pitch. A standard position for the third baseman is approximately three to five feet behind third base and four to six feet off the third-base foul line. Where the third baseman moves from there depends on the batter, count, and game situation. Listed here are a few circumstances that call for third basemen to adjust their positioning.

- *Speedy hitter, less than two outs:* Cheat up on the grass to take away the bunt. If the count gets to two strikes, move a couple of steps back.
- *Double-play situation:* Play even with the third-base bag, and move a step toward second base.
- *Strong, right-handed hitter:* Play a couple of steps deeper in order to increase reaction time and range.
- *Left-handed hitter:* Shift a step or two toward the second-base bag.
- *Late innings holding one- or two-run lead:* Take a step or two to the right to guard the line (from a potential extra-base hit).
- *Runner on third base, less than two outs:* Play even with the third-base bag.

Ready Position

As the pitcher begins his delivery, the third baseman prepares himself in the ready position. Like every defensive position on the field, the third baseman must assume every pitched ball will be hit to him. As the ball is released, the third baseman should take a jab or creeper step forward to ensure he has his weight on the balls of his feet and a slight forward lean with his upper body.

107

> I was never very fast. But you don't need speed for third; you need quickness. I always had more range than other third basemen because my first two steps were quick, that's all.
> —Graig Nettles, former Yankees Gold Glove third baseman, regarded as one of the all-time best at that position

The ready position for a third baseman is slightly different from the position used by the shortstop and second baseman. As the pitch is delivered, the third baseman should use a wider base (feet farther apart) than the middle infielders. This allows the player to set himself (and his glove) lower to the ground. Because the distance from home plate to third base is short, the third baseman does not have the luxury of time. The third baseman must prepare the glove just above the infield grass to field a hard ground ball.

Backhand Plays

The ability to make backhand plays obviously helps third basemen field balls to their right, but it also increases their range on balls to their left. Once players become proficient at using the backhand, they'll feel comfortable playing a little farther off the line. This may enable them to cut off potential base hits destined for the shortstop hole. The backhand is used when the fielders do not have time to get their body in front of the ball. Hard-hit balls just to the player's right or slower hit balls several steps to the right call for the backhand play to be made.

The backhand play can be fielded off (just outside of) the left foot or just inside of the right foot. The pace and distance to the right of the hit often dictates to which foot the ball is fielded. Most players have a preference (right foot or left foot), but there will be situations when the play happens so fast there isn't time to set up to the preferred foot. Infielders should practice fielding backhands off the right and left foot.

Outside the Left Foot

This technique is more frequently used for deep backhand plays that require longer throws. When fielding off the left foot, the final

The third baseman fields every ball he can get to his left. This is a much easier play for the third baseman to make. The shortstop (shown behind) would have to backhand the ball and make a much longer throw.

The third baseman executes a backhand play by fielding the ball outside of his left foot. He then takes a crossover step with his right foot to plant and throw.

step is a crossover step left over right. The fielder bends deep at the knees to lower his body to the ball. He then turns his glove over and reaches across his body. The glove, open as wide as possible, is held just in front of the left foot. The fingers point down and graze the dirt, palm facing the ball. The third baseman should keep his nose behind the glove and attempt to catch the ball in the webbing, rather than the palm. Once in position, he should watch the ball into the glove and squeeze the glove shut as the ball enters.

After the ball is received, fielders have two options regarding their footwork to make the throw. If it's a play where they've stopped their momentum going right before fielding the ball, they can rise up, turn their body toward the target, step with the left foot to the base they're throwing, and fire. If their momentum is still moving right, they should take an extra step and plant their right foot, turn to the target, step with the left foot, and throw. Planting with the right foot provides a strong base to gather balance before unleashing a long throw.

Inside the Right Foot

This technique is more frequently used for shorter backhand plays. To execute the backhand play inside the right foot, the final step is a jab step with the right foot. The player bends deep at the knees and reaches to field the ball just inside the right foot. After the ball is fielded, he pushes up off the right foot to gather balance. He transfers the ball from glove to hand, steps toward the target, and throws. This method is also preferable in double-play situations. It takes less time and is conducive to shorter throws.

Bending deep at the knees is critical whether the player is fielding outside the left foot or inside the right. Players commonly bend at the waist, which makes this play much more difficult. For starters, it's not an athletic position from which to make a tough play. Furthermore, the eyes are farther from the ball and the glove often doesn't quite reach the ground, allowing the ball to slip underneath or bounce off the glove's fingertips. Players should be reminded to bend deep at the knees as they reach for the ball.

Slow Rollers

Two of the common mistakes hitters make is that they (1) get out on their front foot and reach for the ball, and (2) pull up and out

On this slow roller, the third baseman fields the ball outside of his left foot with one hand and throws off his left foot. This is the simpler method and requires an additional step.

of their swing and ascend prematurely into their follow-through. When right-handed hitters make this mistake, they often clip the top of the ball and produce a slow roller to the third baseman. This is one of the toughest plays for the third baseman. The only way to record the out on a slow roller to third base is to field the ball and throw on the run. The feet must keep moving throughout the play. If the fielder stops to set in the fielder's position and then throw, the runner will beat the throw nearly every time.

There are two methods of making this play. The first is a little easier for young players to master. As they approach the ball, they'll field it with the glove hand only. The ball should be received just outside of the left foot. As the right foot lands, the ball is transferred from the glove to the throwing hand. The player

The more advanced method of fielding slow rollers is to field the ball inside the left foot with two hands. The third baseman then steps forward with the right foot and throws (off the wrong foot).

then takes a second step with the left foot and makes the throw to first base.

The second method is more advanced because the second step is eliminated. The third baseman charges the ball and fields it with two hands just inside the right foot. At the time the ball is fielded, the left foot is in front of the right foot. As the right foot steps forward, the infielder brings his hands up for a three-quarter delivery and releases as the right foot plants. This play happens all in one motion. The player actually throws off the wrong foot.

As mentioned, the first method is easier to execute, but it takes longer. However, the fielder will be able to deliver a stronger throw by taking the extra step. The second method is quicker, but the throw won't have as much on it. Regardless of which method is used, the third baseman should concentrate on throwing to the left side of the base. The throw will tail to the right, so this must be factored in when taking aim.

Bunt Coverage

Any time a runner is on first base, or first and second base with less than two outs, the third baseman should be on the alert for a possible bunt. Most sacrifice bunts occur with nobody out, but coaches have been known to move a runner into scoring position with one out. Keep in mind that with a runner on first base and one out, it takes two base hits to score the runner. Many coaches feel there is a better chance of scoring the runner with a sacrifice bunt and one base hit.

With a runner on first base in a bunt situation, the third baseman should immediately charge up on the grass. It is his responsibility to cover any bunt to the left of the pitcher's mound. If the ball is bunted and the third baseman fields it, the catcher should call out where the ball is to be thrown. This allows the third base-man to concentrate on execution: fielding the ball clean and mak-ing an accurate throw. The third baseman must trust his catcher and listen to direction.

Charge means charge! Once the batter shows bunt, the third baseman should eat up as much ground as possible. The quicker the ball is fielded, the better the chance of cutting down the lead runner. Even if there ends up being no play on the lead runner, field-ing the ball quickly increases the time to get the out at first base.

If the ball is thrown to first base, the third baseman should immediately retreat back to third base. The lead runner may attempt to catch him sleeping and run from first to third. The short-stop may come around and cover third base when the third base-man fields the ball, but it's best to not "assume" and to get into the habit of immediately returning to the base.

With runners on second, or first and second base, there must be communication between the third baseman and pitcher. Usually, the third baseman will charge and the shortstop comes in behind to cover third base. However, some pitchers are very athletic and the coach tells the pitcher to cover the left side of the infield (espe-cially if the pitcher is left-handed), allowing the third baseman to remain at the base for the potential force (or tag).

If the pitcher covers the left side, the third baseman remains at third base. If not, he charges and the shortstop covers third. Usu-ally, the play is to second or first base in this situation. It is rare that the play is made at third, unless the ball is bunted very hard. Whatever the case, listen to the catcher's call—he can see the entire field.

Double Plays

A typical 5-4-3 double play (third to second to first) relies on quick-ness and accuracy. The third baseman must field and deliver the

THROW TO THE BASE, NOT YOUR TEAMMATE

There is a lot of movement on bunt plays. The first and third basemen are often charging in. The second baseman moves over to cover first, and the shortstop covers second or third base. At times, the player covering may not yet be at the base when the fielder is ready to throw. The fielder may see that the ball must be thrown immediately in order to get the runner. When this happens, the fielder should lead his teammate with a throw to the base, trusting he will eventually get to the base, catch the ball, and record the out. The fielder should not throw the ball to his teammate. This is a common mistake that results in overthrows or players being safe at first on sacrifice bunts.

ball to second without hesitation. The throw must be accurate in order for the second baseman to receive and redirect the throw to first base.

In a double-play situation, the third baseman moves even with the bag and shades slightly toward second base. On a ball hit directly at or to the left of the third baseman, he should field the ball, remain in his athletic stance, and make a three-quarter delivery throw to second base. This means that he should *not* (1) stand up out of his fielding position before throwing, or (2) drop his throwing arm down and circle up to an over-the-top delivery. These are two common practices that take too much time. A short jab step with the left foot toward second base is all the player needs to make the throw. Taking too many steps before the throw is another common fault that increases the time it takes to deliver the ball.

It's more difficult to turn double plays on balls hit to the third baseman's right. On this play, the third baseman should use his right foot to plant and stop his momentum from moving away from second base. Because it's a longer throw, an overhand delivery may be necessary to record the out at second base.

Throws should be directed to the chest of the player covering second base. This provides him the best opportunity to receive the throw and redirect the ball to first base to complete the double play. Should the second baseman be slightly late covering, the ball should be thrown to the base (chest-high). The first out is vital, and the third baseman must deliver the ball in time to get the lead runner at second base.

On a double-play feed, the third baseman fields the ball and quickly aligns his feet and shoulders to second base. He shouldn't "stand up" to throw the ball, but rather stay athletic and release a quick throw to the base.

Relay Throws

On all throws from left field to home plate, the third baseman must immediately shift into position to provide a cutoff for the left fielder. With an opposing runner on second base, for example, the third baseman becomes the cutoff man on a base hit to left field. The precise positioning is a combined effort between the catcher and third baseman.

The catcher aligns the third baseman (who is facing the outfielder) with the left fielder and home plate. The third baseman listens to the call of the catcher and adjusts accordingly. If the catcher yells, "Left! Left! Left!" the third baseman shuffles to the left until the catcher ceases directing. If he yells, "Right! Right! Right!" he shuffles to the right.

The depth of positioning depends on two factors: how shallow or deep the left fielder gloves the ball, and the strength of his arm. It's essential that the third baseman is aware of how well his teammate throws. Move farther out if the left fielder has a weak arm, and drop back deeper if the outfielder has a strong arm.

As the third baseman sets up for the throw, he should hold his arms up in the air for the left fielder. He does not square up and face the left fielder. Instead, teach him to drop his left foot back and open up slightly toward his glove side. The third baseman should make every effort to catch the ball on his glove side. This saves time when redirecting the throw to home plate.

Once the ball is in flight, the third baseman again listens to the direction of the catcher. If the catcher says nothing, it's the third baseman's responsibility to let the ball go. He should not touch it! It means the throw is a good one and on path to cutting down the runner at the plate. If the ball is to be intercepted, the catcher will yell, "Cut!" The command, "Cut four!" means cut the ball off and immediately throw home. The command, "Cut two!" means cut

The third baseman serves as the cutoff man on throws from left field to home plate. He should open himself slightly to the left to quicken his catch and throw home.

the ball off and immediately throw to second base. The ball is always received with two hands. This assists in transferring the ball from the glove to the throwing hand.

Not every ball will be thrown perfectly. Some throws will be short, long, left, or right. The third baseman must quickly respond to errant throws by adjusting his position when he notices that the ball in flight is off-line. He does not have to hold his line. If the throw is off-line to his right, the third baseman should move to the right as the ball is in flight to force the ball to be on his left side when receiving. On balls thrown short, the third baseman moves up to try to catch the ball before it hits the ground, and on deep throws the player drops back.

Drills

Two Knees, One Glove

The third baseman sets up on his knees. He holds his glove out front in the ready position. Using a tennis ball or IncrediBall (a soft baseball), a coach hits ground balls at the third baseman from approximately 30 feet. The third baseman attempts to field each ball with just his glove hand. This drill teaches and improves a third baseman's skills at reacting to a hard-hit ground ball. Many times, a third baseman doesn't have time to move his feet and must rely on his glove hand to make the play.

Slow Rollers

With the third baseman playing a regular depth, a coach hits slow ground balls to third base. The coach should vary the location: directly at the third baseman, to his left, and to his right. The third baseman charges, fields the ball, and makes the throw on the run.

He must make this play six consecutive times (without mistake) to move on to the next drill.

Web Gems

Playing at various depths, the third baseman alternates fielding ground balls down the third-base line and to the shortstop hole. The purpose of this drill is twofold. First, the third baseman practices executing his technique on balls to his backhand (down the line) and balls far to his left. Second, the third baseman develops a sense of what he can get to in relation to how deep he's playing. For example, if a third baseman is playing deep and knows he can easily cover a ball down the line, he can shade a step or two more to the left to increase his range in the shortstop hole.

In addition, the third baseman gets to practice making great plays so he's polished at producing web gems during the game.

9

THE SECOND BASEMAN

Middle infielders are typically the most sure-handed players on the field. Their responsibilities on the field are many: ground ball fielding, double-play turns, tag plays, cutoff and relay throws, rundowns, and so on. Second basemen should be quick, agile players, who are reliable with the glove and think on their feet. They do not need a powerful arm, but should be accurate with their throws and employ a quick release.

The best feature about playing second base is that players are able to showcase their range and have only a short throw to complete the out. In addition, a second baseman can knock a ball down or bobble it and still have time to throw out the runner at first base. It's a luxury that the shortstop does not enjoy.

Positioning

The second baseman will judge when to change his lateral position (left to right) by considering who is on the mound and who is at the plate. For example, with a slow pitcher on the mound and a right-handed batter, the second baseman shades toward second base. The next hitter might be left-handed, so he shades a few steps to his left. Another factor is the range of the first baseman. A first baseman who has good range to his right enables the second baseman to shade up the middle.

Most important is that the second baseman maintains depth at his position. Because the throw to first base is short, the second baseman can play deeper to increase range. The farther back he plays, the more balls he can get to. Only a few situations call for the second baseman to shorten his depth. He moves up when the double play is in order, in a bunt situation, to defend a play at the plate (infield up on the grass), or if a very fast runner is up at bat. He should also do so when there is high grass in the infield. In this case, the entire infield should shorten their depth because the pace of each hit will be slowed by the grass.

Double Plays

Double plays are difficult to turn at the Little League level, but not impossible. A lot of things need to go right, but if executed properly, a "twin-killing" is a real possibility. Because there is a very short amount of time to turn a double play, the "little things" require particular attention. Each little thing adds up to a big play in the field.

The first step a second baseman must take in a double-play situation is to adjust his position. He must move a few steps forward and a few steps over toward second base. True, this decreases his range on balls hit to the right side of the infield, but he's making this move to prepare for balls to the left side of the infield. Moving up and over enables the second baseman to get to the base quickly, which is a prerequisite to consistently turning double plays. The second baseman should be awaiting the feed from the shortstop or third baseman, rather than arriving at the base as or after the ball is thrown.

Hall of Fame second baseman Napoleon Lajoie had this to say about turning double plays from second base: "I instinctively start for the base as soon as I see the ball is hit to the right of me. It pays to be at the bag in time to help the throw from short or third, for a fraction of a second will lose a double play."

The significance of this point cannot be overestimated. The second baseman must get to the base immediately on a ground ball to

The second baseman needs to get to the bag on a force play as quickly as possible. This enables him to react to an errant throw and/or make a quick double-play turn.

123

the left side of the infield. If the shortstop or third baseman is forced to delay his throw, forget it. Any chance of a double play is lost. Even if the second baseman gets to the base as the ball arrives, it's still not good enough. Catching a ball with your momentum moving toward second base and then redirecting a throw to first base is an unrealistic expectation. In addition, an errant throw by the shortstop or third baseman will be nearly impossible to handle when trying to make the play on the run. A defense must get the first out on a double-play ball, and to achieve that consistently, the second baseman must be at the base early and under control.

Double-Play Turns

Step number one for turning the double play is get to the base. The second baseman makes life a lot easier on himself by getting to the bag immediately. It gives him time to gain balance and get his body in position to make a quick catch and throw.

A key element regardless of the double-play pivot employed is how the ball is received. Footwork is important, but time is also gained or lost because of how the hands are used. Three key points regarding the hands should be stressed when practicing double-play turns:

1. Reach for the ball. The sooner the ball is received, the better. Reaching, rather than holding the glove too close to the body, also frees the hands to work fluidly.
2. Catch the ball in the palm of the glove. This decreases time in transferring the ball from glove to hand. If the ball is caught in the web, the throwing hand must dig the ball out.
3. Catch the ball with two hands. This ensures the first out and also decreases time in transferring the ball from glove to hand. The only time to use one hand is when the ball is thrown wildly.

There are a variety of pivots a second baseman can use to turn a double play. A good suggestion is to have him experiment with each to find what works best. Some turns are simple, while others are more advanced. For purposes of this book, the most basic and safest double-play turns will be discussed. A double-play turn is exciting to see at the Little League level, but it's important to keep young players out of harm's way.

As the player advances, he will also learn to allow the location of the feed to dictate the pivot method he employs. In other words, as the second baseman observes the location of the incoming throw, he decides what pivot to utilize. At Little League age, however, players will execute the turn more consistently if they have a predetermined method in mind.

Across the Bag. Coming across the bag to make the double-play turn is best for ground balls hit at and to the right of the shortstop, or for any ground ball hit to the third baseman. The purpose of coming across the base is twofold. First, the second baseman receives the ball sooner. The second baseman wants to receive the ball as soon as possible on longer feeds (delivered from the third baseman or balls to the shortstop's right). Second, it takes him out of the path of the runner sliding into the base.

As soon as the ball is hit to the left side of the infield, the second baseman sprints to the base. As he approaches the base, he applies the brakes and gets himself under control. He then places his left foot on top of the base and waits to the see the flight of the throw. If the throw is on target, he steps over the base with his right foot and catches the ball as his right foot hits the ground. (Timing this correctly takes practice.) The right foot acts as the plant foot. He then takes a short step in the direction of first base and makes the throw.

When coming across the bag to make the double-play turn, the second baseman steps on the bag with his left foot. He lands hard on his right foot as he receives the throw, squares his shoulders to first base, steps, and throws.

Middle infielders should always keep in mind that they're allowed to "cheat" on any double-play turn. They are not required to have their foot in contact with the base as the ball is received to record the out. The umpire allows them the flexibility to vacate the base prematurely (within reason) to protect the infielder from the incoming runner.

Behind the Bag (Right-Field Side). On balls hit at or to the left of the shortstop, the second baseman presses his left foot against the right-field side of the base. Once he sees that the throw is on target, he pushes back off the base with his left foot. He catches the ball as his right foot hits the ground. His right leg accepts the weight of his body, he steps to first base with his left foot, and he delivers the throw.

Stepping back from the base takes the second baseman out of the path of the sliding runner. The right leg is important in accepting the weight and then shifting the body's momentum toward first base. Often second basemen will not plant and throw, falling back with their weight on their heels. This is a common mistake that leads to weak and errant throws.

Behind the Bag (Left-Field Side). This pivot is best used on balls hit to the shortstop's left in the hole. The second baseman gets to the base quickly and places his left foot on the left-field side of the base. Once he recognizes that the throw is on target, he pushes off the base with his left foot to his right and slightly back. He pushes in the direction of left-center field. The ball is received as the right foot hits the ground. His right leg accepts the weight of his body, he steps to first base with his left foot, and he fires a throw.

Double-Play Feeds

Double-play feeds are used when the ball is hit to the second baseman, and they start the potential 4-6-3 double play. There are three

When stepping back toward the right-field side, the second baseman positions his left foot on the bag. As he receives the ball, he pushes back with his left foot and lands hard on his right foot. He then squares his shoulders to first base, steps, and throws.

When stepping back toward the left-field side, the second baseman positions his left foot on the bag. As he receives the ball, he pushes to the right with his left foot and lands hard on his right foot. He shifts his weight toward first base, steps, and throws.

basic types of double-play feeds: a short, overhand throw; an underhand toss; and a reverse pivot and throw.

Short, Overhand Throws. The most common double-play feed is the short, overhand throw. It is used on balls hit directly at the second baseman, slightly to his left, or slightly to his right. Once the ball is gloved, the second baseman employs an abbreviated arm-swing back and delivers a firm throw to the shortstop's chest.

The footwork can vary on short, overhand throws. On balls hit directly at or slightly to the right of the second baseman, his feet stay planted in the fielding position. He simply turns his left knee inward and drops it down. This will square his upper body to the target. He then brings his arm up and delivers a firm throw to second base.

This double-play feed is used on shorter throws. The second baseman fields the ball, drops his left knee, and turns his body to second base. He delivers a quick, overhand throw to the shortstop.

On balls hit directly at or slightly to the left of the second base-man, he fields the ball, quickly shifts his feet, and aligns them to the target. (The right foot swings back to the right, and the left foot plants and points to second base.) With the shoulders now aligned to the base, the second baseman delivers a crisp, overhand throw to the chest of the shortstop.

Underhand Toss. When the ball is hit close to the second-base bag, the second baseman should use an underhand toss. It's quicker and more efficient. Throwing a ball overhand from a very short distance can be difficult to handle for the shortstop.

After the ball is received, the second baseman remains low to the ground. He then takes a stride with the left foot directly toward second base. The player delivers a firm underhand toss that travels on a straight line to the shortstop's chest. There should be no

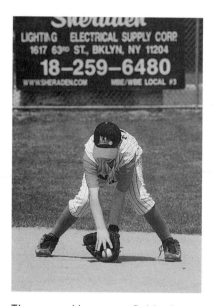 

The second baseman fields the ground ball first, quickly shifts his feet to line up with second base, and makes a crisp feed to the shortstop.

arc in the toss. After the ball is released, the second baseman should follow the throw with his body by taking an additional step with the right foot. The key is to be deliberate with the toss. Let the shortstop see the ball for as long as possible. Again, keep the ball on a line and follow the toss.

Reverse Pivot. This is the most difficult of the double-play feeds. On balls hit far to the second baseman's left, he'll use a reverse pivot. After the ball is gloved, he continues his momentum away from second base and takes a crossover step with the right foot. He plants hard on his right foot to stop his momentum, aligns his shoulders to the target, and fires a strong throw to second base. This is a tough play and requires practice. The shortstop should be set outside the base on this play. This gives the second baseman a

When executing an underhand toss, the second baseman must be deliberate. He steps directly toward second base and delivers a firm underhand toss to the chest of the shortstop.

On balls that take the second baseman far to his left, he uses a reverse pivot to execute the double-play feed. He fields the ball outside of his left foot, crosses over and plants with his right foot, squares his shoulders to second base, and throws.

clear throwing lane. Setting up inside the base risks throwing into the path of the runner.

Bunt Coverage

On nearly every sacrifice bunt play, it is the responsibility of the second baseman to cover first base. With the first baseman charging in to field a potential bunt down the first-base line, the second baseman takes the throws at first base. A coach may opt to have the first baseman stay at first base if he has an athletic pitcher on the mound. In this case the second baseman backs up the throw to first.

On balls bunted to the left side of the infield, the second baseman gets to the base as quickly as possible and squares up to the player delivering the throw. The second baseman positions his right heel on the corner of the base and keeps his left foot on the ground beside his right. Once the ball is released and he sees the flight of the throw, he then steps with his left foot to the throw. As first basemen are taught, he should not stretch before the ball is thrown. It limits ranges on errant throws. After receiving the ball, he should hop off the bag in case any runners attempt to advance.

Balls bunted to the first-base side are fielded by the first baseman, catcher, or pitcher. It is essential that the second baseman give his teammate a throwing lane. He should set up to the inside of the base and stand on the infield side of the bag. He must take this position or risk a potential errant throw or one that hits the runner. The second baseman presses the outside of his left foot against the inside of the base. He stands with his feet shoulder-width apart and holds his arms up to give his teammate a confident target.

Cutoffs and Relays

When a ball is hit over the left fielder's head or into the gap between left and center, the shortstop runs out to become the cutoff man. The second baseman covers second and helps communicate where the ball is to be thrown (if at all) once the shortstop receives the throw. It's best to listen to the command of the catcher and then call out that command to the shortstop.

On balls hit over the right fielder's head or into the right-center-field gap, the second baseman runs out to become the cutoff man. How far the second baseman runs into the outfield depends on the depth of the hit and the strength of the outfielder's arm. As the second baseman moves out for the cutoff, he should occasionally peek over his shoulder at the base runners to get an idea of where the ball will be thrown. He aligns himself as best he can between the

On deep balls hit to the right side of second base, the second baseman provides a cutoff for the right fielder or center fielder. He should listen to the calls of his fellow infielders to determine where to throw the ball once it's received.

outfielder and potential target base. As he awaits the throw, he raises his arms and opens his body slightly to the left.

How the ball is received is important to a quick relay throw to the infield. The second baseman should always try to receive the throw with two hands on his glove side. He takes a short drop step with his left foot and turns and throws to the base called out by his teammates. If the ball is thrown to the second baseman's right (throwing side), he should move to the right and force the ball to his glove side as it's received. A quick transition from catch to throw is a skill that could be the difference between the runner being safe or out.

A fly ball over center field requires communication between the shortstop and second baseman. Commonly, if it's over the center fielder's head to the shortstop side, the shortstop becomes the cut-off man and vice versa. If it's directly over his head, the shortstop and second baseman must immediately inform each other as to who is going and who is covering second. Shortstops usually have the stronger arm of the two, and consequently take the throw in this situation.

Covering the Steal

Communication between the shortstop and second baseman is very important in steal situations. It's essential because the coverage may change from batter to batter. If a right-handed batter appears likely to pull the ball, the second baseman covers second base on the steal and the shortstop backs up on the play. If the same batter looks late on pitches and more likely to hit to the opposite field, the short-stop covers and the second baseman backs up. The rule of thumb is whomever the ball is more likely to be hit to should hold his ground while his teammate breaks with the runner.

Second basemen are usually cheated toward second base on a steal, because they're already playing at double-play depth (except with two outs). This helps them get to the base quickly. When the runner breaks, the second baseman sprints over and straddles the base. The right foot is on the home-plate side of second base and the left foot is on the center-field side of second base. The second baseman stands in an athletic position, glove held toward the catcher.

As the ball arrives, the second baseman receives it with one hand, and in a fluid motion, swipes his glove across the dirt in front of second base. After the tag is applied, he keeps his glove moving upward and shows the umpire the ball. On tag plays, the player

On a tag play, the second baseman receives the ball and gets his glove "in and out" on the tag. After applying the tag, he should immediately show the umpire the ball.

wants to get his glove in and out. He should not rest his glove in front of the base, because that affords the base runner an opportunity to knock the ball loose. Even if the throw beats the runner handily, the second baseman should hold his glove above the base and apply a swipe tag as the runner arrives. Again, his glove should be in and out and shown to the umpire.

If the shortstop is covering the steal, the second baseman waits to see that the ball is not hit and then takes a deep route behind second base to back up the throw. The second baseman keeps enough distance between second base and where he's stationed to allow him time to react to an errant throw.

DOUBLE-PLAY BALL BACK TO THE PITCHER

The second baseman and shortstop must communicate about who is covering second base on balls hit back to the pitcher. Typically, the shortstop will take the throw because it's an easier double-play turn for him to make. But perhaps the infield is shaded to the left and the second baseman is much closer to the bag. Before a pitch is thrown, the shortstop, second baseman, and pitcher should collaborate on who is covering second base on a ball back to the pitcher in a double-play situation. The second baseman and shortstop decide and alert the pitcher. "Me and you on a double play," the second baseman might say, followed by pointing to the pitcher and then himself.

Drills

Feeds and Turns

With a teammate covering second, the second baseman fields balls to his right, left, and directly at him, and works on his double-play feeds. Balls should be hit sharply, softly, and routinely so the second baseman develops instinct in deciding what feed is the correct one to employ.

From the shortstop and third-base positions, a coach throws balls to the shortstop covering second base to practice double-play turns. Balls should be thrown on-target, high, wide, and short. Through repetition, the second baseman must become adept at handling anything that comes his way during competition.

Quick Exchange

The second baseman and a fellow middle infielder stand 15 feet apart in an athletic position. The object is to throw the ball back and forth, concentrating on transferring the ball from glove to hand as quickly as possible and making a firm, accurate return throw.

137

Instruct players to develop a rhythm in which they're catching the ball, transferring it from glove to hand, and making a return throw all in one motion. Use a stopwatch to see how long it takes to throw the ball back and forth 15 times. Each practice, players should attempt to beat their best time.

Short-Hop Picks

Two players stand approximately 10 feet apart. Each positions his feet wide apart and bends deep at the knees with his rear end low to the ground and his glove extended out. They make short-hop throws back and forth to each other. (A short hop is a ball that hits the ground just in front of the player's reach.) Players do not move their feet in this drill, but rather isolate their glove hand to work on picking balls. This drill pays dividends when fielding batted balls, receiving throws on steals, executing double plays, and fielding throws from the outfield. A second baseman can make a great play that also rescues a teammate who made a low throw.

10

THE SHORTSTOP

No infield position is more difficult to play than shortstop. It requires a variety of physical skills such as agility, quickness, and arm strength. It's a very unforgiving position, in that any mistake leaves virtually no time for recovery. The shortstop is involved in nearly every play on the field and can make or break a game in any number of ways.

Taking these factors into consideration, it's no surprise that a team's best defensive player can generally be found at the shortstop position. Shortstops must be physically gifted, poised, instinctive, and sometimes creative. Future Hall of Fame shortstop Cal Ripken Jr. possessed these gifts but also augmented his talents by absorbing information to anticipate the play before it happened. "I like to learn their hitters and our pitchers and cheat a little bit and cut down the area I have to cover," he once said. "I'm not blessed with the kind of range a lot of shortstops have. The way I have success, I guess, is thinking."

Fielding Through the Ball

Infielders are often instructed to charge ground balls rather than wait back on their heels. There is no position where this is more significant than shortstop. Shortstops simply do not have the luxury of time. It's the position that is farthest from home plate. Distance takes time, and if a shortstop rests on his laurels awaiting the ground ball, he gives the batter an excellent chance of beating the throw to first base.

As mentioned in Chapter 3, shortstops should practice fielding through the ball on routine ground balls. Instead of charging the ball and stopping to set their feet in the traditional fielder's position, shortstops must keep their feet and momentum moving through the ball. This reduces the distance of the throw to first base and allows them to glove the ball sooner.

Shortstops first circle around the ball so they're fielding it with their momentum moving in the direction of first base. This may require a step or two to the right on balls hit at or to the right of the shortstop. As they approach the ball, they set their left foot out in front of their right foot. They reach out with their glove and throwing hand, fielding the ball just off the inside of their right foot. They then take a shuffle step and fire to first base.

On a slow roller, shortstops take the same approach. But after fielding the ball, they take a short step with their right foot and throw off the wrong foot (which is the right foot). Catching and throwing, then are executed in a fluid, continuous motion.

140

Positioning

Much like the second baseman, the shortstop adjusts his lateral positioning based on the hitter and pitcher. Is the batter more likely to hit the ball to the left or right side of the infield? Once the shortstop arrives at an educated guess, he shades accordingly.

Depth is equally important. Some shortstops make the mistake of playing too deep. Sure, it increases range, but it also makes every play close at first base. This forces shortstops into the habit of rushing, which causes a variety of problems. A shortstop with a strong

The shortstop charges the ball at a controlled pace. He fields the ball with two hands just inside his right foot. He keeps his feet moving, squares up to first base, and delivers an accurate throw.

arm can afford to play a little deeper, but even strong-armed short-stops need to minimize their depth with a fleet-footed and/or left-handed hitter at the plate.

The shortstop has large holes both to his right and left. Should he be fortunate enough to play alongside a third baseman who has great range, he can cheat more toward the hole up the middle. Scott Rolen is a prime example of an exceptional defensive third base-man who makes his shortstop even better. He has great range to his left, which allows his shortstops to expand their range up the middle. Rolen also takes away a lot of difficult backhand plays for his shortstops.

Game situations also influence where the shortstop assumes his ready position. When the double play is in order, he'll move a few steps up and over toward second base. He'll move up on the grass to defend the play at the plate. Also, he may play halfway with a

When a shortstop likes to play deep, it is essential that he charges and fields through ground balls.

runner on third base. This means he'll play midway between "up" on the grass and regular depth. On hard-hit balls, he'll throw home if the runner goes. On slow rollers or a ball taking him to his right, he'll get the out at first even if the runner breaks for home.

Double Plays

Nothing is more devastating to an offense than when the defense turns a double play. Two outs are recorded on one swing, and a once-promising inning is quickly thwarted by the opposition. The shortstop is involved in double-play turns at second base on every ground ball hit except for those fielded by the third baseman. Balls fielded by the catcher, pitcher (usually), second baseman, and first baseman are thrown to the shortstop covering second base. Obviously, a shortstop starts a double play by giving a feed to the second baseman on ground balls hit to him.

Double-Play Feeds

The shortstop delivers the ball to second base using a method that is dictated by the location of the hit. Always remind the shortstop to be quick, not to rush. Too often the play breaks down when the shortstop thinks about making the feed before he has cleanly secured the ball in his glove. He should field it first, and then make a quick, accurate throw to the second baseman's chest.

On balls hit directly at or just to the left of the shortstop, he simply pivots and throws to second base. He fields the ball and remains in a low, athletic position. (The shortstop should not stand up to make the throw. It wastes time.) The left and right foot pivot to point toward second base; he keeps his shoulders level and turns to second base to make a firm, overhand throw.

The shortstop must follow through on his throw. A common mistake is to tense up on short throws and try to guide the ball.

This causes errant throws that are difficult for the second baseman to handle. Focusing on the follow-through keeps the delivery fluid.

The type of feed employed on a ball hit to the shortstop's right or backhand largely depends on arm strength. Some players are able to field the ball, shift their weight to their right leg to load up, and throw the ball sidearm to second base without taking a step. This is the quickest method, but it entails a strong arm and accuracy.

For most Little League players fielding a ball to their right, it's best to receive the ball, gain balance, and then take a quick shuffle step and throw to second base. It takes a little more time, but it ensures getting that all-important first out.

On balls hit far to the left of the shortstop, an underhand toss is the best feed to use. The player stays low to the ground, steps toward second base with the left foot, and delivers a firm under-

On double-play feeds, the shortstop should stay low (athletic) after fielding the ball. Often, shortstops stand upright before releasing the ball and lose time on the play.

hand toss to the second baseman's chest. There is no arc to the throw, and the shortstop follows the throw by stepping forward with the right foot after release. It should be very deliberate and allow the second baseman to see the ball as long as possible.

There will be times when the shortstop fields the ball very close to second base. In this case, he should take the play himself. He should hold on to the ball, step on the base with the left foot, and fire to first for an unassisted double play. If one step (the feed) can be eliminated, the shortstop should take it himself by all means. It's a quicker turn and lessens the chance for error.

145

On balls hit to the shortstop's left, he should deliver an underhand toss to the second baseman. He steps at second base and is deliberate with the toss.

Double-Play Turns

The double-play turn is an easier task from the shortstop position than it is from second base. The advantage a shortstop has is momentum. As he approaches second base, he is nearly squared up to the target. A second baseman has to redirect his throw to first base.

Like the second baseman, the shortstop should get to the base as quickly as possible on a double-play ball. Arriving late to the base hinders the shortstop's ability to execute a quick turn and handle errant throws. The approach to the base must have depth, meaning the shortstop rounds off his route to the back of second base. Rather than running a straight line to the base and having to shift clockwise to align the feet and shoulders to first base, the shortstop bows his approach to the center-field side of the base. This enables him to receive the ball with his body squared to the target. On certain plays, the shortstop won't have the luxury of time to elongate his route to second base, but if time allows, he should add depth on his approach to the base.

There are two basic double-play pivots from the shortstop position: inside the bag and outside the bag. The shortstop receives feeds from the second baseman, first baseman, pitcher, and catcher. To whom and/or where the ball is hit determines which pivot is employed.

Pivot Outside the Bag. This pivot is used on routine and hard-hit ground balls hit to the second baseman. It is also used on ground balls fielded by the first baseman when he's playing deep. When using this pivot, the shortstop runs to the back corner of the second base. As the ball is delivered, he steps to the ball with his left foot. He drags his right foot on the back corner of the base as he comes across to catch the ball. After the ball is received, he takes a short, shuffle step with his left foot to align his feet and shoulders to first base and delivers the throw.

Receiving the ball outside the base takes the shortstop away from the path of the runner. He must slide his foot across only the rear corner. He does not have to step on top of the base, just merely clip the back of the bag. The shortstop must align his shoulders with first base to consistently deliver an accurate throw. Often the shoulders point left of the target and induce errant throws to the right and left of the first baseman.

147

On the double-play turn, the shortstop gets to the base quickly. His right foot rests on (or just behind) the back side of the base. Once he sees the throw is accurate, he shifts to the left of the base to receive the ball and get out of the runner's way. He then squares his shoulders and throws to first base.

Pivot Inside the Bag. This pivot is used on ground balls to the pitcher or to the first baseman when he's up or in front of the base, and on bunt plays fielded by the catcher or the first or third baseman. It's also used on slow rollers to the second baseman when he fields the ball in front of the runner. To set up for the inside pivot, the shortstop approaches the inside (infield side) of the base. He steps on the rear inside corner of the base as he catches the ball. The shortstop then pushes off to the right with his left foot. This takes him out of the path of the runner. He lands on his right foot, steps with the left, and fires to first base.

On double plays started by the first baseman, it's extremely important that the shortstop give the first baseman a target inside the baseline. It provides the first baseman with a clear throwing

When the first baseman fields the ball near the infield grass, the shortstop must provide a target inside the base. If he remains centered over second base, the first baseman has a difficult throw that may hit the runner.

lane and avoids the risk of hitting the runner with the throw. It's a bad habit for a shortstop to approach the back of the base on throws from the pitcher or on bunt plays. And here's the reason. If a teammate uncorks a low throw, it may hit the base if the shortstop is positioned on the back side of the base. The shortstop needs to get in front of the base to receive the ball sooner, and to have a chance to pick low throws out of the dirt.

149

On a double-play feed from the pitcher or catcher, the shortstop positions himself in front of the base to make the double-play turn. This allows him to receive the ball sooner and also provides an opportunity to pick a low throw out of the dirt.

Bunt Coverage

With a runner on first base, the shortstop covers second base on bunt plays. He sets up inside the base in hopes of turning a double play. If there is no chance of a double play, the shortstop takes the mind-set of a first baseman when receiving the throw. His job is to make sure an out is recorded.

The sacrifice bunt will also be in order with a runner on second base or first and second base. In these game situations, the shortstop looks to the head coach to signal what coverage is on. With runners on first and second, the coach may have the third baseman charge and the shortstop cover third base for a possible force at third. This is called a "rotation coverage." The shortstop must run to cover third base as soon as the batter shows bunt and second base is left open. Another coverage calls for the pitcher to cover the third-base side, allowing the third baseman to remain at third base. If this is the case, the shortstop covers second base. Whatever the play call, the shortstop is always moving in a bunt situation. It's important that the entire infield is alerted to the bunt coverage before the pitcher toes the rubber.

Cutoffs and Relays

For any balls hit over the right fielder's head or into the gap between right and center field, the second baseman runs out to become the cutoff man. The shortstop covers second base and helps communicate where the ball is to be thrown (if at all) once the second baseman receives the throw. It's best to listen to the command of the catcher and then reinforce his command by calling out over and over to the second baseman.

On balls hit over the left fielder's head or into the left-center-field gap, the shortstop runs out to become the cutoff man. How far the

> *When you talk about coming across the bag on a double play, you've got to be able to improvise, because that guy bearing down on you is never going to be in the same place two times in a row.*
>
> —Ozzie Smith, Hall of Fame shortstop

shortstop runs into the outfield depends on the depth of the hit and the strength of the outfielder's arm. As the shortstop moves out for the cutoff, he should occasionally peek over his shoulder at the base runners to get an idea of where the ball will be thrown. He aligns himself as best he can between the outfielder and potential target base. As he awaits the throw, he raises his arms and opens his body slightly to the left.

How the ball is received is important to a quick relay throw to the infield. The shortstop should always try to receive the throw with two hands on his glove side. He takes a short drop step with his left foot, turns, and throws to the base called out by his teammates. If the ball is thrown to the shortstop's right (throwing side), he should move to the right and force the ball to his glove side as it's received. A quick transition from catch to throw is a skill that could be the difference in the runner being safe or out.

A fly ball over the center fielder requires communication between the shortstop and second baseman. Commonly, if it's over the center fielder's head to the shortstop side, the shortstop becomes the cutoff man and vice versa. If it's directly over his head, the shortstop and second baseman must immediately inform each other as to which one of them is going and which one of them is covering second. Shortstops usually have the stronger arm of the two and consequently take the throw in this situation.

Covering the Steal

Communication between the shortstop and second baseman is very important in steal situations. It's essential because the coverage may change from batter to batter. If a right-handed batter appears likely to pull the ball, the second baseman covers second base on the steal and the shortstop backs up on the play. If the same batter looks late on pitches and more likely to hit to the opposite field, the shortstop covers and the second baseman backs up. The rule of thumb is that whomever the ball is more likely to be hit to should hold his ground while his teammate breaks with the runner.

Shortstops are usually cheated toward second base on a steal, because they're already playing at double-play depth. This helps them get to the base quickly. When the runner breaks, the shortstop sprints over and to the back of base. The right foot is on the home-plate side of second base and the left foot is on the center-field side of second base. The shortstop stands in an athletic position, glove held toward the catcher.

152

As the ball arrives, the shortstop receives it with one hand, and in a fluid motion, swipes his glove across the dirt in front of second base. After the tag is applied, he keeps his glove moving upward and shows the umpire the ball. On tag plays, the player wants to get his glove in and out. He should not rest his glove in front of the base, because he affords the base runner an opportunity to knock the ball loose. Even if the throw beats the runner handily, the shortstop should hold his glove above the base and apply a swipe tag as the runner arrives. Again, his glove should be in and out and shown to the umpire.

If the second baseman is covering the steal, the shortstop waits to see that the ball is not hit and then takes a deep route behind second base to back up the throw. The shortstop keeps enough distance between second base and where he's stationed to allow him time to react to an errant throw.

Infield Pop-Ups

Among outfielders, the center fielder has priority over the wing out-fielders. The shortstop has priority over all infielders. On infield pop-ups, the shortstop must be accountable and aggressive in making plays. He can be an invaluable source of outs on these plays that help the pitcher and his team. There are two plays in particular that the shortstop should practice: a pop fly over the third baseman's head that's destined for shallow left field, and a pop-up over second base in short center field.

The ball over third base is an easier play for the shortstop than for the third baseman. He has a better angle to the ball. As soon as the ball goes up, the shortstop takes a drop step with his right foot and runs for the ball. If he sees he can get to the ball, he should call for it so the third baseman gets out of the way. Of course, if the left fielder calls for the ball, the shortstop peels off. Outfielders always have priority over infielders.

The ball over second base is an easier play for the shortstop than for the second baseman because it's to his glove side. Both middle infielders should be aggressive in their pursuit, but if the shortstop can get to the ball, he should call for it. If the center fielder calls for the ball, both the shortstop and second baseman should cease their pursuit.

Drills

Round the Ball

Set up five or six cones in a line that first curves slightly to the right and then bends back to the left. The line of cones extends approximately 12 feet in length. With the shortstop positioned at the rear cone, a coach hits routine ground balls to the nearest cone. The shortstop follows the path of cones (to their right), fields the ball

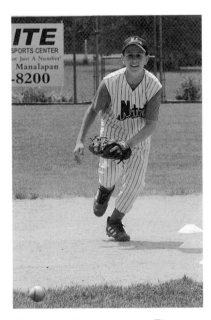

The Round the Ball drill. The shortstop begins at the rear cone. The coach hits a ball toward the front cone. The shortstop must follow the path of cones and hustle to field the ball at the front cone.

This forces him to round the ball and take an angle that will align himself to first base and provide momentum on his throw.

at the first cone, and throws to first base. The ball is fielded just inside the right foot and the feet continue moving as the ball is received.

This drill is designed to teach to the shortstop to round the ball. The cones represent the path taken so the shortstop can align himself with first base and field through the ball.

Quick Exchange

The shortstop and a teammate stand 15 feet apart in an athletic

Quick Exchange is a great drill that develops soft, quick hands.

position. The object is to throw the ball back and forth, concentrating on transferring the ball from glove to hand as quickly as possible and making a firm, accurate return throw.

Instruct players to develop a rhythm in which they're catching the ball, transferring it from glove to hand, and making a return throw, all in one motion. Use a stopwatch to see how long it takes to throw the ball back and forth 15 times. Each practice, players should attempt to beat their best time.

Feeds and Turns

With a teammate covering second base, the shortstop fields balls to his right, left, and directly at him and works on his double-play feeds. Balls should be hit sharply, softly, and routinely so the shortstop develops an instinct for deciding what feed is the correct one to employ.

From the catcher, pitcher, first-base, and second-base positions, a coach throws balls to the shortstop covering second base to practice double-play turns. Balls should be thrown on-target, high, wide, and short. Through repetition, the shortstop must become adept at handling anything that comes his way during competition.

11

THE OUTFIELDERS

In Little League, it's customary that the players with the most advanced skills play the infield positions. It is true that more balls are hit in the infield during a Little League game and infielders have a larger impact on a greater number of plays. But those few plays that outfielders make, good or bad, can have a tremendous impact on a game's outcome. An outfielder can stymie a big rally with a fantastic catch, or he can commit a blunder that opens the floodgates to a devastating inning. Having good outfielders is critical to playing excellent team defense.

When we think of outfielders we think of catching fly balls. This ability is obviously a major aspect of playing an outfield position, but there are numerous additional factors integral to the makeup of a good outfielder. Fielding ground balls, having arm strength, throwing with accuracy, performing reverse pivots, backing up bases, and communicating with infielders represent many of the additional skills that outfielders must possess and practice to be adequate defensively.

General Guidelines for Playing Outfield

The Center Fielder Is Chief

There are subtle differences and responsibilities to each outfield position, but there are also guidelines that every outfielder follows. The first is that the center fielder is the captain of the outfield. Any ball he calls for is his. This means that if the right fielder and center fielder are calling for a fly ball, the right fielder backs off as soon as he hears the center fielder call for the ball. In return for having priority over the right and left fielders, the center fielder backs up his wing outfielders on every play.

Every Ball Is My Ball

That said, all outfielders should exercise the thought that they are going to catch every ball that is hit in the air. An outfielder never assumes that his teammate will catch a fly ball. Good outfielders are hungry for plays and approach the game with eagerness and aggression. With that attitude, each outfielder anticipates that every pitched ball will be hit to him. It's the only way to read the ball quickly and get a good jump. Is it realistic that every pitch is hit to the outfield? Of course not. But the moment an outfielder doesn't expect the ball to be hit to him, it's on its way.

Communication Is a Priority

Outfielders communicate with each other in a variety of ways. Calling for the ball is the most obvious communication. The center fielder often communicates with the right and left fielders by giving them guidance. He may yell, "In! In! In!" or "Back! Back! Back!" The center fielder has the best angle to read how shallow or deep a ball is hit to right and left field.

Any balls that are hit toward outfield or foul-line fences require help from fellow outfielders. Usually, an outfielder is tracking a ball on the run and isn't exactly sure of how much distance he has left before he

Communication is extremely important in the outfield. Players must talk and sometimes use body language. Calling for the ball should be something that is overstated, rather than understated.

gets to a fence. His fellow outfielders can help him by yelling, "You have room! You have room!" or "Fence! Fence! Fence!" This is especially important on balls hit deep toward the outfield fence. Many Little League fields do not have warning tracks, so an outfielder in pursuit of a deep fly ball needs assistance from his teammates.

Know the Weather Conditions

Any time there is wind (even if it's a slight breeze), outfielders should constantly check its direction. Outfielders should continuously reach down, pick up grass, and toss it in the air to determine the wind's strength and direction. The outfielder should factor wind into his positioning and path to a batted ball. Every ball hit in the air will be influenced by wind, and the higher the hit, the more it will be affected.

Right and left fielders should never dive on hard-hit balls hit toward the foul line unless the ball is definitely in foul territory. If the ball is fair and not caught, it's going all the way to the fence and yielding a triple or inside-the-park home run. Balls down the line are too far from the center fielder to rely on him for a backup. The only time it's okay to dive for a ball down the line is if it's a high, lofted ball that won't travel far if it lands safely. Otherwise, don't dive toward the lines.

The position of the sun is another factor that is taken into consideration. Most games are two hours long, so the sun's position will change throughout the game. If the sun is a factor, the outfielder needs to be aware of it before the ball is hit. He can use his glove to block the sun, or, if he has the option, he can wear outfield sunglasses to help him fight the glare.

Dusk is one of the most difficult times to play outfield. It can be tough to see the ball off the bat. In this situation, the outfielder needs his infielders to help him out by pointing to the ball as soon as it's hit. The infielders must be told, however, or they won't know to give assistance.

Back Up Your Teammates

Outfielders should back each other up on every batted ball, both fly balls and ground balls. Outfielders are the last line of defense, and if the ball gets past an outfielder it's going all the way to the fence.

All throws from infielders must be backed up as well. These include throws to first, forces at second, steal plays, pickoffs, and so on. Outfielders are active on all plays in the infield. Backing up a base denies a base runner the chance to advance an extra base, and it can present an opportunity to throw out a runner who attempts to advance.

Pop-Up Priorities

While the center fielder has priority over the left and right fielders, outfielders have priority over all infielders. On shallow pop-ups to the outfield, the infielders and outfielders will chase to make the catch. Because the outfielder is running forward and the ball is in front of him, he has the authority to call off the pursuant infielder(s). As soon as an outfielder opens his mouth, the infielders peel off and get out of the way.

Understanding who has priority is extremely important, not simply to increase the chances of catching the ball, but to ensure safety as well. This particular play can cause nasty collisions between

Each outfielder has priority over every infielder. If the outfielder knows he can catch the ball, he should call for the ball so the infielders can peel off and get out of the way.

players that risk injury. Go over this time and time again in practice so the players understand who has priority and begin to develop trust in one another. This must be practiced for reasons greater than recording outs.

Left Fielder

How to choose which outfielder plays left and which plays right field is often decided by one factor: arm strength. The player to put in left field is the one who has less arm strength. It's not a knock on the outfielder as much as it is common sense. The throw to third base is much shorter for the left fielder, where it's a lengthy throw for the right fielder. You do not want teams running from first to third base on every base hit to right field, so you put the stronger arm in that position.

There are other factors that could come into play. Perhaps a pitching staff has below-average velocity and a lot of balls are pulled to left field. In this case, a coach may want to put his best fielder in left field. Understanding the strengths and weaknesses of the entire roster is important when selecting positions for players.

Left field is an easier position to play for a left-handed player. Most balls hit to left field hook or fade to the left-field line. When a right-handed hitter pulls the ball, he often hits "around" or contacts the outside of the ball causing it to dive toward the foul line. When a left-handed batter hits a ball to left, he commonly slices it and it fades toward the foul line. With a left-handed left fielder, all balls that fall toward the foul line fall to his glove hand. It's a minor issue, but it's an easier play for him to make.

Also, on long throws to home plate, a player's throw often tails—to the playing-field side of home plate from a left-hander and to the foul-territory side of home plate from a right-hander. It makes the play for the catcher more difficult or impossible if the

> *I had a tendency to not read a ball right, particularly when it was hit right at me. So I had to learn not to move, to keep my feet planted for a second before going.*
> —Vince Coleman, former major-eague outfielder

throw tails into the runner. Again, this is a minor issue, but it could make the difference in a game.

The throws from left field to second and third base are short throws. The left fielder should be reminded that if he's going to miss, miss low. Low throws give the infielder a chance to make a play. Throws that are wild high and over the head of the infielder provide him with no chance. If you're going to miss on a throw from the outfield, miss low.

Backing Up

A left fielder is very active on balls that are not hit to him. On ground balls to the third baseman and shortstop, the left fielder takes a path behind the fielder in case of an error or bad hop. Should the ball get past the infielder and the left fielder is daydreaming, an aggressive base runner can take second base.

On double-play balls to the right side of the infield (first and second base), the left fielder backs up the throw to second base. This is critical because the play is right in front of the base runner. If the throw gets past the shortstop and the runner sees the left fielder isn't backing up, he'll immediately continue to third base.

Every throw to third base is backed up by the left fielder: steal plays, bunt plays, rundowns, and so on. Even if a ball is hit to the shortstop and the base runner attempts to advance from second to third base, the left fielder sprints to back up third base. Perhaps the

With a left-handed singles hitter at the plate, the left fielder should play shallow and toward the line. You would be surprised at how many balls are dumped into short left field for base hits by slap-hitting lefties.

It's important to shade toward the left-field line, not just shallow. A ball punched to short left will slice toward the foul line. If the left fielder is already positioned there, the ball will fade right to him. If he's not positioned there, the ball will fade down and away from him, which is a very difficult catch to make.

ball gets past the third baseman, ricochets off the fences, and caroms into short left field. The left fielder has to be there to prevent the runner from scoring.

The left fielder backs up every ball hit to the center fielder. Whether it be a ground ball, line drive, or long-hit fly ball, the left fielder runs over to back up. This accomplishes two things. First, it covers the center fielder if he makes a mistake and the ball gets past him. It doesn't prevent the bleeding, but it stops it. Second, it enables the center fielder to play his position more aggressively. If the center fielder is confident that his wing outfielders are backing him up, he's more apt to take a risk and dive for a ball. Instead of playing it safe and conceding the base hit, he can leave his feet, make a great play, and get an out.

As major-league all-star and Gold Glover Barry Bonds said, "When you back him up, you're giving the other guy room, you're letting him know that you're there for him if he misses the ball. He can be more aggressive, and you've found another way to hold runners, too."

Rounding the Ball and Reverse Pivots

Ground balls hit through the infield offer considerable time for the outfielder to charge the ball and perfect the angle of approach. This is called rounding the ball. For example, say there is nobody on base and the batter strokes a base hit between the shortstop and third baseman. The job of the left fielder is to field the ball and throw to second base. But instead of running straight to the ball, fielding it, and then aligning the feet and shoulders to second base before throwing, the left fielder takes a path to the right side of the ball. He rounds off his route so that as he fields the ball, his body is already in line to throw to second base. Rounding the ball sets the outfielder up for stronger, more accurate throws.

There are hits that don't allow time to round off balls. Hard-hit balls to the gap and down the third-base line may force the left fielder to use a reverse pivot. On balls hit to deep left-center field,

Rather than running straight to a ground ball, this outfielder rounds the ball so he's in line with the base once he gloves the ball. This provides him with momentum to make a strong, accurate throw.

a right-handed left fielder employs a reverse pivot when turning to throw to second base, third base, or the cutoff man. A left-handed left fielder uses a reverse pivot on balls hit deep down the third-base line with the play at second or third base.

As the ball is fielded, a right-handed player takes a crossover step with his right foot. With this step, he turns his back to the infield. The right foot plants, and he aligns his feet and shoulders to the target. A short step is taken with the left foot and the ball is thrown. Using a reverse pivot ensures stronger, more accurate throws.

Right Fielder

The right-field position is very similar to left field. Most balls hit hook or fade toward the foul line. Batted balls by right-handed hitters slice, and fly balls hit by left-handers often hook. The right-field position is slightly easier for right-handed fielders because most fly balls carry toward their glove side.

Some of the best arms in major-league baseball (past and present) have played right field. Right fielders Vladimir Guerrero, Sammy Sosa, Ichiro Suzuki, Jesse Barfield, and Roberto Clemente have showed off some of the greatest throws ever seen on a baseball field. Right field is the "strong-arm" position for outfielders.

Backing Up

The right fielder is very active because he's moving on every throw to first base. Keep in mind that balls carom off fences and may kick into short right field. The right fielder isn't doing anything else on ground balls to the infield, so he may as well back up in case the improbable becomes a reality.

More obvious plays to back up are bunt plays to first base and pickoffs from the catcher and pitcher. The right fielder also backs up all force plays to second thrown from the left side of the infield.

Any throws from the third baseman or shortstop to second base must be backed up.

Last, the right fielder backs up all balls to center field. Most center fielders are sure-handed, but fielders have to expect the unexpected. Right fielders should back up on ground balls, line drives, and fly balls.

Rounding Balls and Reverse Pivots

Much like the left fielder, the right fielder rounds off routine ground balls to the outfield. As the ball is fielded, right fielders should be in line with the base they're throwing to so they build momentum into their throw. A right-handed right fielder employs a reverse pivot on balls hit into the right-field corner. Throws to second base, third base, or the cutoff man are longer when the right fielder fields the ball to his left. Using a reverse pivot increases arm strength and accuracy. Left-handed right fielders may use a reverse pivot on balls hit deep into the right-center-field gap.

It's important that the right fielder gets to the ball quickly and is prepared to come up throwing. Most base runners (or base coaches) are going to test a young outfielder's arm strength and accuracy by attempting to take an extra base. "In right field, what you know is everyone is going to run on you," says former major-league right fielder Jesse Barfield. "The plays you are most often faced with will be challenges to your arm which you just have to answer."

167

Center Fielder

The captain of the outfield, the center fielder is the team's best outfielder. He is the most sure-handed, covers the most ground, possesses a strong arm, and exhibits leadership on the field. The list of center-field greats is impressive: Joe DiMaggio, Willie Mays, Mickey Mantle, Ken Griffey Jr., Torii Hunter. Even lesser-known

OUTFIELD CUTOFFS AND RELAYS

It is very important for outfielders to hit their cutoff men with their throws. Not only can doing this produce outs, but it also stops runners from advancing an extra base. When middle outfielders move out for a cutoff, they will relay your throw to a base for a potential out. If your throw never gets into their hands, the opportunity is lost and the runner is safe. The ball must be thrown on a line to the chest of the middle infielder. Outfielders should not even look at the base runners, but rather focus on hitting the cutoff man with an accurate throw.

When the corner infielders are the cutoff, there is a potential play at the plate. And the word *potential* cannot be emphasized enough. Once the ball is fielded and thrown, there may be no chance at getting the runner. Just because the throw is supposed to go home does not guarantee there is a realistic chance of getting the runner once everything plays out. If the throw is on line to the cutoff man, there may be an opportunity to cut down a different runner on the base paths.

Too often, the outfield misses the cutoff man, leaving no chance to get a runner out. Base runners move up into scoring position and the double play is now taken out of order. Outfielders should focus on throwing the ball through the chest of the cutoff man. This provides a chance for the cutoff man to do what he's there for, cut the ball off.

168

players turned heads while showcasing their amazing speed and athleticism. It was often said about former Philadelphia Phillies center fielder Gary Maddox, "Two-thirds of the earth was covered by water. The rest was covered by Gary Maddox."

The center fielder is rewarded for his talents by having a direct view of the batter. He's reading batted balls from a direct angle, which helps his judgment tremendously. Also, most balls hit toward center field are hit square and lack sidespin. This keeps the flight of the ball true, so the ball doesn't hook or fade away from the center fielder.

Any ball the center fielder knows he can easily catch he should call. He has the best angle and read of anyone on the field. But he needs to understand that he should call every ball he *knows* he can easily catch, not *thinks* he can catch. Center fielders can get into a habit of calling for balls prematurely, negating the opportunity for a wing outfielder or infielder to make an easier play.

Backing Up

The center fielder backs up on ground balls hit to middle infielders, and on all throws to second base. More important, the center fielder backs up his right and left fielder on all plays. It's his responsibility to back up his outfield teammates on every play. If he fails to and they make a mistake, it spells disaster.

Balls Hit Directly at the Center Fielder

While the center fielder gets a great read on the ball and doesn't deal as much with hooking or slicing fly balls, the ball hit directly at the center fielder is a very difficult play. Line drives at the center fielder are tough because it's difficult to judge the depth of the hit. It takes extra time for the center fielder to determine whether he should come in, stay put, or go back for the ball. The best advice for the center fielder is to take that extra time. Don't commit right away. Bend deep at the knees to gain a better perspective on the ball, and wait to react before making a rash decision. The most common mistake is when the center fielder takes a quick step in and the ball beats him over his head. He should wait to get a better read, and then break.

The center fielder should back up his other outfielders on every play.

Long fly balls directly over the center fielder are also tough plays. Deep fly balls to the right or left are simple. The player takes a drop step to the side of the hit, points his toe to where he wants to go, and takes off. On balls hit directly over the top, the center fielder takes a drop step and forces the ball to one side. Which foot he takes a drop step with is a matter of personal preference.

For example, let's say a center fielder is more comfortable taking a drop step with his right foot. On a ball hit directly over his head, he takes his initial drop step with his right foot and instead of running a route straight back, he bows out to the right. This forces the ball to be to his right. He then makes the catch over his right shoulder. Running straight back would force the center fielder to make an over-the-shoulder catch on a ball falling directly overhead. This is very difficult. He should force the ball to one side by taking a rounded route to the point of the ball's descent.

Drills

Fly-Ball Mania

This drill is a lot of fun for outfielders. It's designed to work on drop steps, running laterally for balls, coming in on balls, and throwing.

The outfielder faces the tosser, approximately three feet away. On the call, "Break!" the outfielder takes a drop step to the right. The tosser allows the player to run 30 feet and then tosses the ball over his right shoulder. Immediately after catching the ball, the outfielder must plant his feet, align his body with the tosser, and make a strong return throw. After throwing the ball, the outfielder breaks to his left, running a straight line across. The tosser catches the return throw and delivers a line-drive throw to the outfielder's left that hits him on the run. The outfielder catches the ball, plants (using a reverse pivot if necessary), delivers a strong throw to the

171

Coaches should make sure they give their outfielders plenty of fly balls during practice. It's the only way to develop and improve judgment.

tosser, and then runs directly at the tosser. The tosser catches the return throw and delivers a short fly ball that the outfielder has to catch below the waist on his way in.

Outfielders love this drill, and it works on a variety of skills. After starting the outfielders to their right a few times, start them to their left and reverse the direction of throws.

Batting-Practice Fly Balls

There is no better time to practice judging and catching fly balls than batting practice. It accurately simulates the way a ball comes off the bat in a game. Taking fly balls from a coach tossing them up and hitting them is great practice, but it isn't quite the same as a batter hitting a pitched ball.

Outfielders should take their customary position, or rotate positions if they play more than one spot in the outfield. They should work on weaknesses in order to challenge themselves to get better. For example, if an outfielder has trouble going back on balls, he should play very shallow in batting practice so he'll get more opportunities to go back on balls.

12

TEAM DEFENSE

No single player records an out on the baseball field. Pitchers compile strikeouts but need the catcher to receive strikes. Infielders and outfielders make unassisted plays but rely on the pitcher to entice the batter to swing and put the ball into play. Baseball is a team game, especially on the defensive end.

Certain plays, categorized at "situational plays," arise during a baseball game that require the defensive unit to perform in concert to thwart an offensive attack. All players must be accountable for their individual responsibilities to ensure the defense succeeds. They must know who is covering what base, where the ball should be thrown, who gets involved in the play, who backs up and where, and when the sequence of action is initiated. The entire team must work together because if just one player slips up, the line of defense becomes vulnerable.

These situational plays that surface include bunt coverages, first-and-third steal situations, rundowns, cutoffs, and relays. Each play requires planning, direction, communication, and practice. Players must be coached to execute in these game situations, or they will be taken advantage of on the field. The last thing a coach wants for his players is to have them unprepared for such situations and find themselves at the mercy of the opposing offense.

Bunt Coverage

Defensive bunt coverages are used to defend sacrifice bunts. An offensive team institutes a sacrifice bunt when they're looking to advance a runner already on base. The batter is "sacrificing" himself to move a runner into scoring position. With a runner on first base, a sacrifice bunt advances the base runner to second base, which puts him in position to score on a base hit. With a runner on second base, a sacrifice bunt advances the runner to third base. With less than two outs, a runner on third base can score on a fly ball, ground ball, pass ball, base hit, or wild pitch.

Sacrifice bunts are usually used when the score is close in the latter stages of the game. If a team is up by a run, for example, they may want to add an insurance run. During a tied game, when trailing by a run, or when facing a dominating pitcher are also popular times to sacrifice bunt in an effort to manufacture a run.

174

In a bunt situation, the first baseman plays up on the grass and creeps forward on the pitch.

Runner on First Base

With a runner on first base, the bunt coverage is very simple. The first and third basemen charge toward home plate when the batter squares (or pivots) to bunt. The second baseman breaks to his left to cover first base. The shortstop shifts to his left to cover second base. The pitcher fields any ball that is bunted directly toward him. The catcher fields the ball on short bunts near home plate.

The role of the catcher is vital in bunt situations. Because the catcher is the only position player facing the field, he must commandeer the play and call out which base to throw to. If there is a sure chance of getting the lead runner at second base, the catcher should call out, "Two, Two, Two!" If there is any question about getting the lead runner, take the sure out at first base. "One, One, One!"

Third basemen must be alert to aggressive base runners. If they field the ball and throw to first base on the bunt, they must imme-

In typical bunt coverage, the first baseman charges in to field the ball and the second baseman covers first base. The second baseman should cheat toward first base a bit in a potential bunt situation.

diately retreat back to third base. The lead runner might try to race from first to third if the third baseman fails to cover the base. If another teammate fields the bunt, the third baseman should also retreat back to third base immediately.

Runner on Second Base

There are two basic options to use with a runner on second base. The first is for the first and third basemen to charge and the shortstop to break over to cover third base. The shortstop has to break as soon as the batter shows bunt in order to get to the base in time. The second baseman covers first base, and second base is left open.

It's very difficult to get the lead runner in this situation because there is no force at third base. The ball has to beat the runner by enough to allow the player covering to catch the ball and apply a tag. In most cases, the play is to first base to get the sure out.

The second option is to have the third baseman remain at third base. The pitcher is responsible for covering the third-base side on a bunt, the first baseman charges, the shortstop moves to second base, and the second baseman covers first. This coverage is often used when there is a quick, athletic pitcher on the mound or a left-handed pitcher (because they fall off to the third-base side in their follow-through).

Runners on First and Second Base

There are three basic options for this game situation. Remember, the primary objective is to get an out. Getting a lead runner is a bonus.

The first option is to use the basic coverage. Corners (first and third basemen) charge, the second baseman covers first, the shortstop covers third, and second base is left open. There is a force at third on this play, so the throw does not have to beat the runner by a lot. But the fielder has to be absolutely sure he can make the play or you're looking at bases loaded.

The second option is to have the pitcher cover the third-base side. The third baseman stays at third, the shortstop covers second, and the second baseman covers first. All bases are covered, but it's important to have an agile pitcher.

The third option is to have the pitcher cover the first-base side. The second baseman covers second base, the shortstop shifts to third, and the third baseman charges. This is called the "rotation" play.

There are two things to keep in mind when coaching bunt coverages. First, the primary objective is to get an out. The opposition is sacrificing an out to advance runners, so your team must take

A good third baseman charges aggressively on bunt plays. If he fields the ball quickly enough, he may have a chance to throw out the lead runner on the play.

advantage of that sacrifice. Second, the catcher must be vocal. The catcher can see the play develop in front of him, and he is the field general.

Communication

Which bunt coverage to execute is the decision of the coach. The coach must relay this information to a player, who then gives a sign to the rest of the infield. The two players most commonly used to relay signals are the catcher and third baseman. Whichever player is used, the coach should have a set of signs for the chosen player that communicates the coverage to be implemented. The player then gives a signal to the infield before the pitcher toes the rubber.

It's very important that the player giving the sign has everyone's attention. The coach should look to see that all eyes are on the catcher (or third baseman). The sign can be verbal, but the best method is to have the player go through a series of nonverbal signals. That way, the coach can see that all players are watching, and not be concerned that a player never heard the sign.

First-and-Third Steals

Runners are on first and third with one out. The batter takes the pitch and the runner on first breaks to steal second base. The catcher throws to second, and upon release the runner on third breaks for home and scores easily. This is a staple play in Little League baseball and is indefensible unless the defensive team is prepared.

Listed here are several options to defend this game situation:

- Go for the runner at second base. If your catcher has a good arm and your team is in a position to trade an out for a run, get the out.

- Fake the throw to second base and try to pick the runner off third base. The runner on third may break too early and find himself in no-man's-land on a fake throw.
- The pitcher cuts the ball off. The catcher gets up and throws as if he's throwing to second. (The catcher should aim for the pitcher's head.) The pitcher spears the ball and quickly throws to third (or home) to cut down the lead runner.
- Throw the ball to the shortstop breaking in toward home plate. This gives the runner (and third-base coach) the impression that the ball is being thrown all the way to second. With the shortstop breaking in, it shortens the distance of the throw and provides a very good chance of throwing the runner out at home plate.
- Throw the ball to the second baseman breaking in toward home plate—same rationale as already stated.
- Let the runner take second base. If you have confidence in your pitcher and defense, concentrate on getting the batter and avoid throwing the ball around.

Work on two to four of these play options in practice. They must be practiced over and over so kids will know exactly what to do during competition. Also, make sure everyone on the team (infielders, outfielders, and pitchers alike) knows the plays. You never know who will be playing where at any given time.

When the situation arises in the game, there are several factors a coach must consider when calling a play. The score may be such that you're willing to concede a run to get an out, so you'd throw through to get the runner stealing. Conversely, the score may influence you to concede the steal and defend the runner at third.

Other factors to consider are the speed of the runners at first and third and also who you have playing at each position. Perhaps the catcher and shortstops have strong arms, so you'll consider run-

On this first-and-third steal, the play call is for the shortstop to run in front of second base and cut off the throw. If the runner from third breaks, the shortstop fires home to get the out.

180

ning the play where the shortstop breaks in and cuts the ball off. The catcher may have a weak arm, so you may attempt to have the pitcher cut off the throw. Whatever you decide to call, have a verbal or nonverbal sign for each play. When time is called, give the sign to the catcher and have the catcher walk in front of home plate and signal the play to the infield. Vary your plays throughout the game.

Rundowns

If there is any play on the baseball field that most likens itself to a circus act, it has to be the rundown. It's entertaining to watch and fun for kids, but it usually ends in disaster for the defensive team. The number-one infraction committed on this play: too many throws. The more throws by Little League players, the greater the chance of the ball being dropped or thrown away. Runner is safe! Limit the number of throws and increase your chances of tagging out the runner.

To limit the number of throws, the defensive player with the ball has to make the runner commit to running to a base. The way to do that is to run at the base runner hard! Force the runner to make a decision. If the runner tries to dance around in the middle, the defensive player running hard will tag the runner out. If the base runner runs hard to a base, the defensive player can then toss the ball to his teammate at the base, who will receive the ball and tag the runner out. Getting the base runner to run hard toward one base prevents him from stopping, turning around, and running in the opposite direction.

When running at the base runner hard, the defensive players should hold the ball in their throwing hand and hold it up high. This is so their teammate at the base can see the ball. Defensive players should not fake their throws in an effort to fool the runner. They'll end up fooling their own teammate, and when they actually deliver the throw, the teammate will be caught off guard and possibly miss the throw.

One other quick point: the player holding the base must give his teammate a throwing lane. This means that he should never stand in a direct line with the runner. It makes the throw nearly impossible for his teammate, giving him the sole option of lofting a throw over the head of the runner. That is much too difficult and usually

In a rundown, the player with the ball must get the base runner running hard so he's forced to commit. The player holds the ball high so his teammate can easily see a potential throw.

results in the ball being thrown wild high. The defensive player holding the base should move to one side or the other to give his teammate a clear target to throw to. Also, the player holding the base should shorten the distance of the rundown by coming in off the base. There is no rule that says the fielders have to stay at their base. Reduce the distance and suffocate the runner. Work on this in practice. If you don't, it will haunt you in the game. Kids enjoy this drill, so it's not difficult to maintain their attention.

Cutoffs and Relays

With a runner on second base, a single to the outfield often creates a play at home plate. Little League outfielders may not have the arm strength to reach the plate from the outfield and may need the help of a teammate. Infielders must be cutoffs if a throw needs to be relayed home or thrown to an alternative base.

On balls hit to left field, the third baseman is the cutoff. He should position himself from up near the edge of the infield dirt to back deeper in the infield grass. Exactly where he stands depends on the depth of the outfielder and the strength of his arm. On balls hit to center and right field, the first baseman becomes the cutoff. His positioning also depends on the outfielder's depth and arm strength.

The catcher must be vocal on this play. If the throw is strong and on-line, he should say nothing. No command means the ball goes untouched and continues its path to home plate. If the ball is off-line or is losing steam, the catcher should yell, "Cut!" The word that follows cut dictates where the ball is thrown. "Cut four!" means the cutoff player should throw home. "Cut two!" means the throw goes to second base, and so on. If the catcher simply yells, "Cut!" the cutoff player holds the ball and checks the runners on base.

On extra-base hits, the middle infielders become cutoffs for the outfielders. They run out into the outfield grass, raise their hands, and listen for the catcher's call of where the throw should go. On balls hit to left field, the shortstop is the cutoff player. On balls hit to right field, the second baseman is the cutoff player. If the ball is hit to center field, the middle infielder with the stronger arm (usually the shortstop) becomes the cutoff player. Practicing this will not only get your team some outs during the season but will also stop the opponent from taking extra bases. This will pay major dividends over the course of a season.

183

Infield/Outfield Practice

Infield/outfield practice should be implemented into every practice and pregame routine. It places players at their fielding positions all at one time and enables them to practice game situations. For pregame routine especially, a crisp infield/outfield practice can set the tone for the game.

Outfield

Hit to the outfielders first in infield/outfield practice. Left fielders should throw to second base, and the center and right fielders should throw to third base. Hit two ground balls to the left fielder, one directly at the fielder and one to his right. Emphasize accurate throws to the base. Second basemen should receive the throw at second base from the left fielder; first basemen should back up the throw.

Hit two ground balls to the center fielder. Hit the first directly at the player and the second to his left or right. The shortstop acts as the cutoff man on the throw and should be aligned directly between third base and the position where the center fielder gloves the ball. It's the responsibility of the third baseman to line up the shortstop for the cutoff. A pitcher should run off the mound and back up third base.

Hit two ground balls to the right fielder. Hit the first directly at the player and the second to the player's right. Emphasize accurate throws to the base. The shortstop acts as the cutoff man and (again) is lined up by the third baseman. The second baseman covers second base, and a pitcher should run from the mound and back up third base.

The second round of balls hit to the outfield are thrown home. Hit a ground ball to the left fielder followed by a high fly ball. On throws home from left field, the third baseman acts as the cutoff man, the shortstop covers third base, and the second baseman covers second base. The catcher aligns the third baseman between home plate and the origin of the throw. A pitcher should back up home plate.

A crisp infield/outfield practice can set the tone for a good game.

On balls thrown home from center and right field, the first baseman is the cutoff man. The catcher aligns the first baseman with the throw while the third baseman covers third, the shortstop covers second, and the pitcher backs up home plate. First base is left open.

After you've completed the second round of hitting balls to the outfield, have an assistant coach trot out to the foul line with a fungo bat and baseballs. All outfielders should move toward center field and shag fly balls. Have the assistant hit balls to the outfielders while you continue with infield practice.

Infield

A crisp infield practice can solidify a great practice or set the tone for a game. Promote high standards during infield practice so that

Here, the infield is playing up to defend a play at the plate. Each player is up on the infield grass.

players elevate their concentration. Especially entering a game, you want players coming off the field feeling good about the game they are about to play.

The first round of ground balls is hit directly to the player and thrown to first base. Hit a routine ground ball to the third baseman, shortstop, second baseman, and first baseman, and then roll a bunt out for the catcher to field and throw to first. Hit balls to the infielder's left during the second round of ground balls. Again, the play is to first base.

Call out, "Let's get two!" for the third and fourth round of ground balls. The second baseman covers the base on ground balls hit to third base and shortstop, receives the throw, and then fires to first base to complete the double play. The shortstop covers second base on ground balls hit to the second baseman, first baseman, and catcher. Hit the first round of double-play balls directly at the

In this formation, the corners (first and third baseman) are up, but the middle infielders are back at double-play depth.

position player and the second round of double-play balls to his left or right. (Force him to react.)

For the final round, call out, "One and in!" Have each fielder back up a few steps and play deep. Hit a ground ball to the fielder's right to force a long throw to first base. After he makes the throw to first, the fielder should move forward to play a second ground ball. This ball should be fielded and fired home for a tag play at the plate. Repeat this for each fielder at third base, shortstop, second base, and first base. After the first baseman has completed his throw to the plate (and if you're really good), hit a foul pop-up to the catcher to complete infield/outfield practice. Hitting a high pop to the catcher isn't as hard as it seems. Toss the ball up high and look to slice under the backside of the ball with a severe uppercut. The best way to learn is through trial and error.

Bibliography

Bench, Johnny. *The Complete Idiot's Guide to Baseball*. New York: Alpha, 1999.

Delmonico, Rod. *Defensive Baseball*. Indianapolis, IN: Masters Press, 1996.

Falkner, David. *Nine Sides of the Diamond*. New York: Simon and Schuster, 1999.

Gola, Mark. *The Little League Guide to Conditioning and Training*. New York: McGraw-Hill, 2004.

Gola, Mark. *Winning Softball for Girls*. New York: Facts on File, 2002.

Voorhees, Randy. *Coaching the Little League Pitcher*. New York: McGraw-Hill, 2004.

Voorhees, Randy, and Mark Gola. *As Koufax Said*. New York: McGraw-Hill, 2003.

Index

Anticipation, pitchers and, 57
Around-the-horn drill, 103–4

Backhand plays
  for ground balls, 37–39
  third basemen and, 108–11
Backing up
  center fielders and, 169
  left fielders and, 163–64
  pitchers and, 69–70
  right fielders and, 166–67
Balls in the dirt, first basemen and,
    96–97
Batting-practice fly balls, outfielders
    and, 172
Belanger, Mark, 16
Blocking pitches, catchers and, 78–79
Bonds, Barry, 164
Bunts, 115
  catchers and, 83–85
  communication and, 178
  defensive coverage for, 174–78
  first basemen and, 100
  pitchers and, 65–67, 71
  second basemen and, 131–32
  shortstops and, 150
  third basemen and, 113–14

Catchers
  blocking pitches and, 78–79
  characteristics of good, 73–74
  defending steals and, 80–83
  drills for, 88–89

fielding bunts and, 83–85
framing pitches and, 76–77
pop-ups and, 86–87
receiving pitches and, 74–76
stance for, 74, 75
Catching, 15–17. *See also* Throws
  drills for, 26–27
  eliminating fear of, 20
  form, 17–19
Center fielders, 167–69. *See also*
      Outfielders
  backing up and, 169
  balls hit directly at, 169–70
  as captain, 158
Coaches
  injured pitchers and, 61
  responsibilities of, 12–13
Coleman, Vince, 163
Communication
  bunt coverage and, 178
  outfielders and, 158–59
  pitchers and, 57–58
Counting bounces drills, 43
Cutoffs
  defensive coverage for, 182–83
  outfielders and, 168
  second basemen and, 132–33
  shortstops and, 150–51

Defensive playing
  building team pride with, 8
  forcing opponents to adjust with, 7–8
  good, teams and, 2–8

importance of, 1–2
pitchers and, 7, 58
poor, team pride and, 12–13
poor, teams and, 9–12
Defensive training, 1
DiMaggio, Joe, 167
Do-or-die method, for outfield ground
    balls, 41
Double plays
    feeding
            second basemen and, 126–31
            shortstops and, 143–45
    second basemen and, 122–31
    second basemen and shortstops in,
        137
    shortstops and, 143–49
    third basemen and, 114–16
    turning
            second basemen and, 123–26
            shortstops and, 146–49
Drills. *See also* Practice
    for catchers, 88–89
    for catching and throwing, 26–27
    for first basemen, 103–4
    for fly balls, 54–55
    for ground balls, 42–43
    for infielders, 185–87
    for outfielders, 184–85
    for pitchers, 71
    for second basemen, 137–38
    for shortstops, 153–56
    for third basemen, 119–20
Dusk, playing outfield during, 160

Evans, Dwight, 96

Falkner, David, 91
Fastballs
    four-seam, 21
    two-seam, 21
Fear, eliminating
    of catching, 20
    of fly balls, 45–47
Feeding double plays
    drills for, 137, 155–56
    second basemen and, 126–31
    shortstops and, 143–45

Fences, fly balls and, 51–53
Fielding drills, for pitchers, 71
Fielding fundamentals, for ground balls,
    33–37
First base cleanup drills, 104
First basemen. *See also* Infielders
    balls in the dirt and, 96–97
    bunts and, 100
    drills for, 103–4
    importance of, 91–92
    positioning for, 93–94
    receiving throws and, 94–96
    relay throws and, 101–3
    throws to second base and, 98–100
First-and-third steals, defensive
    coverage for, 178–80
First-base cleanup drill, 104
Fly balls. *See also* Ground balls
    batting-practice, outfielders and,
        172
    catching, 48–49
    developing judgment for, 47–48
    drills for, 54–55
    drop steps for, 50–51
    eliminating fear of, 45–47
    fences and, 51–53
    going back on, 49
Fly-balls-coming-in drill, *55*
Fly-ball mania drills, 171–72
Four-seam grip, 21
Framing pitches, catchers and, 76–77

Game-of-21 drill, 26–27
Griffey, Ken, Jr., 167
Grips
    for balls, 20–21
    four-seam, 21
    two-seam, 21
Ground balls, 29–30. *See also* Fly balls
    advanced method for fielding, 42
    backhand plays for, 37–39
    "creeper step" for, 32–33
    drills for, 42–43
    fielding fundamentals for, 33–37
    outfielders and, 40–41
    pitchers and, 59–65
    preparing for, 32–33

proper positioning for, 30–32
"ready position" for, 32

Hitting, 1
Hold Programs, pitchers and, 68–69
Huggins, Miller, 74
Hunter, Torii, 167

Infielders. *See also* First basemen;
    Outfielders; Second basemen;
    Shortstops; Third basemen
    positions for, for outfield ground
        balls, 40
    practice for, 186–88

Jeter, Derek, 42
Jump pivot method, 80, 81

Kaat, Jim, 70
Knockout game, 71

Lajoie, Napoleon, 123
Left fielders. *See also* Outfielders
    backing up and, 163–64
    reverse pivots and, 165–66
    rounding off balls and, 165
    selecting, 162
Line drives, pitchers and, 59
Long toss drills, 27

Maddox, Gary, 168
Mantle, Mickey, 167
Mays, Willie, 167

Nettles, Graig, 107

Observation, pitchers and, 57
Offense, minimizing changes of,
    3–5
One-knee drills, for throwing, 26
One-knee position, for outfield ground
        balls, 40–41
"Out" opportunities, 2
    big innings and, 4–5
Outfielders, 157. *See also* Center
    fielders; Infielders; Left fielders;
    Right fielders

communication and, 158–59
cutoffs and, 168
drills for, 171–72
general guidelines for, 158–62
ground balls and, 40–41
pop-up priorities for, 161–62
practice for, 184–86
relays and, 168
tips for, 49
weather conditions and, 159–60
Overhand/underhand fly ball drills, 54

Pendleton, Terry, 105
Pickoff plays, second basemen and, 133
Pickup drills, 43
Pitchers
    anticipation and, 57
    backing up bases and, 69–70
    bunting and, 65–67
    coaches and injured, 61
    communication and, 57–58
    defense and, 58
    defensive playing and, 7
    double-play balls back to, 137
    fielding drills for, 71
    fielding ground balls and, 59
    ground balls to right side of infield
        and, 63–65
    ground balls with bases empty and,
        59–60
    ground balls with runners on bases
        and, 60–63
    Hold Program for, 68–69
    line drives and, 59
    observation and, 57
    poor defensive playing and, 10–11
    pop-ups and, 67
    strikes and, 5–7
Pitches
    blocking, 78–79
    catchers and, 74–76
    framing, 76–77
Pitching, 1
Playing. *See* Defensive playing
Pop-ups
    catchers and, 86–87
    pitchers and, 67

priorities for, outfielders and,
  161–62
shortstops and, 153
Practice. *See also* Drills
  for infielders, 185–87
  for outfielders, 184–85
Pride, team. *See also* Teams
  good defensive playing and, 8
  poor defensive playing and, 12–13

Quarterback/wide receiver drill, 54–55
Quick-exchange drills
  for second basemen, 137
  for shortstops, 154–55
Quick-feet drill, 88

Relay throws. *See also* Throws
  defensive coverage for, 183–84
  first basemen and, 101–3
  outfielders and, 168
  second basemen and, 133–34
  shortstops and, 151
  third basemen and, 117–19
Reverse pivots
  left fielders and, 165–66
  right fielders and, 167
Right fielders, 166. *See also* Outfielders
  backing up and, 166–67
  reverse pivots and, 167
  rounding off balls and, 167
Ripken, Cal, Jr., 139
Rocker step method, 80, 82
Round-the-ball drill, for shortstops,
  153–54
Rounding off balls
  left fielders and, 165
  right fielders and, 167
Routine plays, 4
Rundown drill, 71
Rundowns, defensive coverage for,
  181–82

Schmidt, Mike, 4
Second basemen. *See also* Infielders
  bunts and, 131–32
  characteristics of good, 121
  covering steals and, 134–36

cutoffs and, 132–33
double plays and, 122–31
double-play balls back to pitcher and,
  136
drills for, 137–38
pickoff plays and, 133
positioning for, 121–22
relay throws and, 132–34
Short-hop picks drill, 137
Shortstops. *See also* Infielders
  bunts and, 150
  characteristics of good, 139
  covering steals and, 152
  double plays and, 143–49
  double-play balls back to pitcher and,
    136
  drills for, 153–56
  fielding ground balls and, 42
  fielding through the ball and, 139–40
  pop-ups and, 153
  positioning for, 140–43
Situational plays, 173
Slow rollers, third basemen and,
  111–13
  drills for, 119–20
Smith, Ozzie, 3, 151
Squeeze plays, pitchers and, 67
Steals
  covering
    second basemen and,
      134–36
    shortstops and, 152
  defending, catchers and, 80–83
  first-and- third, defensive coverage
    for, 178–80
Strikes
pitchers and, 5–7
umpires and, 76
Sun, position of, playing outfield and,
  160

Teams. *See also* Pride, team
  defensive playing for building pride
    for, 8
  defensive playing for helping, 2–8
  defensive plays for, 173–88
  poor defensive playing and, 9–13

Third basemen. *See also* Infielders
    backhand plays and, 108–11
    bunts and, 113–14
    characteristics of good, 105–6
    double plays and, 114–16
    drills for, 119–20
    positioning for, 106–8
    relay throws and, 117–19
    slow rollers and, 111–13
Throws, 16. *See also* Catching; Relay
        throws
    accuracy and, 24–26
    drills for, 26–27
    firing, 23–24
    form for, 19–24
    initiating, 21–23
    receiving, first basemen and, 94–96
    relay, first basemen and, 101–3
    to second, first basemen and, 98–100

Tips, for outfielders, 49
Training. *See* Defensive training
Turning double plays
    drills for, 137, 155–56
    second basemen and, 123–26
    shortstops and, 146–49
21, game of, drill, 26–27
Two knees, one glove drill, 119
Two-seam fastballs, 21

Umpires, 76
Underhand/overhand fly balls drill, 54

Weather conditions, outfielders and,
        159–60
Web-gems drill, 120
Wide receiver drill, 54–55

About the Author

Mark Gola has written several sports instructional books, including *The Little League Guide to Conditioning and Training* (2004), *As Koufax Said* (2003), and *The Louisville Slugger Complete Book of Hitting Faults and Fixes* (2000). Gola, a former northeast regional All-American baseball player at Rider University, was an assistant baseball coach at Rider and Princeton University. He is currently a professional baseball instructor at Dave Gallagher's All-American Baseball Academy. He lives in Robbinsville, New Jersey.